MARRIAGE IN CULTURE

MARRIAGE IN CULTURE

Practice and Meaning
across Diverse Societies

JANICE E. STOCKARD

THOMSON

WADSWORTH

Australia • Canada • Mexico • Singapore • Spain • United Kingdom • United States

Publisher	Earl McPeek
Acquisitions Editor	Bryan Leake
Developmental Editor	Lynn McGarvin
Market Strategist	Katie Matthews
Project Manager	Elaine Hellmund

Cover photo: Thomas L. Kelly

ISBN-13: 978-0-15-506386-0
ISBN-10: 0-15-506386-3
Library of Congress Catalog Card Number: 2001091869

Wadsworth/Thomson Learning
10 Davis Drive
Belmont CA 94002-3098
USA

For information about our products, contact us:
Thomson Learning Academic Resource Center
1-800-423-0563
http://www.wadsworth.com

For permission to use material from this text, contact us by
Web: http://www.thomsonrights.com
Fax: 1-800-730-2215
Phone: 1-800-730-2214

Printed in the United States of America
10 9 8 7 6 5 4

■

Contents

Illustration Credits   vii
Preface   ix
Acknowledgments   xi

1   MARRIAGE AS A CULTURAL PRACTICE   1
A South China Illustration   3
Creating a Gendered Perspective on Marriage:
The Effects of Kinship and Residence Practices   5
Of Marriage and Theory   8
Marriage in Four Cultures: Selection and Sequence   10

2   MARRIAGE AMONG THE !KUNG SAN OF SOUTHERN AFRICA   12
Hunting and Marriage   15
The Challenge of the Egalitarian   15
Of Men, Women, and the Division of Labor   16
Band and Family, Camp and Kin   18
Reciprocity and Social Life   22
Mobility and Subsistence   25
Men, Women, and Conflict   26
To Earn a Wife: Passage to Manhood and Brideservice   28
Marriage, Parity, and Politics   30
Residence and the Relatively Egalitarian Life   33

3 MARRIAGE IN TRADITIONAL CHINESE SOCIETY   38
Of Husbands and Plows   41
Male Descent Lines and Marriage   43
To Arrange a Marriage   46
Brides and Lines   48
The Wife in the House That Marriage Built   51
Polygyny: More as Better   53

4 MARRIAGE AMONG THE HISTORICAL IROQUOIS   58
The Iroquois in History   60
Horticulture and the Divisions of Labor in Kinship   64
Of Longhouses and Female Descent Lines   65
Kinship, Marriage, and Politics   68
Residence and the Meaning of Marriage   72
Brothers and Sisters, Husbands and Wives   79

5 MARRIAGE AMONG TIBETANS: THE NYINBA OF NEPAL   81
Polyandry in Agrarian Society   83
Of Houses and Lines   84
The Organization of Work in Marriage   87
The Dynamics of Polyandry   88
Sons and Fathers   89
Exceptions to Polyandry   93
Marriage, Hierarchy, and Identity   97

Epilogue   101
Notes   107
References   119

Illustration Credits

Map 1.1.   Manuel Lizarralde
Figure 1.1.   Reprinted, by permission, FormAsia Books, Ltd.
Map 2.1.   Manuel Lizarralde
Figure 2.1.   Marshall Family Collection
Figure 2.2.   Marshall Family Collection
Figure 2.3.   Marshall Family Collection
Figure 2.4.   Marshall Family Collection
Figure 2.5.   Marshall Family Collection
Figure 2.6.   Patricia J. Wynne
Figure 2.7.   Marshall Family Collection
Figure 2.8.   Marshall Family Collection
Figure 3.1.   Courtesy Peabody Essex Museum, Salem, Massachusetts (negative A9195)
Figure 3.2.   Courtesy of The Government of the Hong Kong Special Administrative Region
Figure 3.3.   Reprinted from John Stuart Thomson, *The Chinese* (Bobbs-Merrill, 1909)
Figure 3.4.   Reprinted from John Stuart Thomson, *The Chinese* (Bobbs-Merrill, 1909)
Figure 3.5.   Courtesy of Valery M. Garrett, *Chinese Clothing: An Illustrated Guide* (Hong Kong: Oxford University Press, 1994)
Figure 3.6.   James P. Warfield
Figure 3.7.   James P. Warfield
Figure 3.8.   James P. Warfield
Figure 3.9.   James P. Warfield
Map 4.1.   Manuel Lizarralde

Figure 4.1.   Illustration by Richard H. Pease for Lewis H. Morgan, *League of the Ho De' No Sau Ne, or Iroquois* (Rochester: Sage & Brother, 1851)

Figure 4.2.   Illustration by Richard H. Pease for Lewis H. Morgan, *League of the Ho De' No Sau Ne, or Iroquois* (Rochester: Sage & Brother, 1851)

Figure 4.3.   Used with permission from *America's Fascinating Indian Heritage*, copyright 1978 by the Reader's Digest Association, Inc., Pleasantville, New York, www.readersdigest.com. Illustration p. 123 by Vic Kalin.

Figure 4.4.   William Fenton, courtesy of the American Philosophical Society

Figure 4.5.   William Fenton, courtesy of the American Philosophical Society

Figure 4.6.   Frank Speck, courtesy of the American Philosophical Society

Figure 4.7.   William Fenton, courtesy of the American Philosophical Society

Figure 4.8.   William Fenton, courtesy of the American Philosophical Society

Figure 4.9.   William Fenton, courtesy of the American Philosophical Society

Figure 4.10.   William Fenton, courtesy of the American Philosophical Society

Figure 4.11.   William Fenton, courtesy of the American Philosophical Society

Map 5.1.   Manuel Lizarralde

Figure 5.1.   Thomas L. Kelly

Figure 5.2.   Thomas L. Kelly

Figure 5.3.   Thomas L. Kelly

Figure 5.4.   Reprinted, by permission, from Nancy Levine, *The Dynamics of Polyandry: Kinship, Domesticity, and Population on the Tibetan Border*, p. 104. Copyright 1988 by The University of Chicago.

Figure 5.5.   Thomas L. Kelly

Figure 5.6.   Thomas L. Kelly

Figure 5.7.   Thomas L. Kelly

Figure 5.8.   Thomas L. Kelly

Figure 5.9.   Thomas L. Kelly

Figure 5.10.   Thomas L. Kelly

Preface

The idea that became *Marriage in Culture* had its origins in the many classrooms at Stanford University, San Francisco State University, and Connecticut College where I have taught anthropology. In those classrooms, my focus was marriage (along with the related topics of family, kinship, and gender) within one or several cross-cultural settings. Although students seemed to find the subject of marriage almost inherently compelling, the ethnographies and edited volumes available for classroom use seemed too often written for an exclusive audience of professional anthropologists. I wanted a book that could be used as a core integrating text, one that could facilitate the use of traditional anthropological literature, as well as provide a ready platform for a cross-cultural comparative analysis of marriage.

I conceived *Marriage in Culture* as just such a core integrating text, designed for classroom use across a wide variety of disciplines, including anthropology, sociology, history, feminist studies, ethnic studies, and marriage-and-family courses. It introduces students to the rich insights that anthropology offers into the meaning of marriage in radically different societies. Chapters focus on marriage within !Kung San (Bushman), Chinese, Iroquois, and Tibetan societies. *Marriage in Culture* also familiarizes students with the anthropologist's unique perspective on culture, each chapter placing marriage within the context of the whole culture, exploring the ways in which different economic, political, kinship, family, and gender systems and ideologies shape the practice of marriage and its meaning.

Marriage in Culture is also intended to facilitate the analysis of the practice and meaning of marriage in the United States and more broadly, to encourage an appreciation of marriage everywhere as a product of specific cultures and histories.

■

Acknowledgments

I wish to acknowledge the intellectual and theoretical inspirations made to the present work by anthropologists whose work has defined the contemporary field of marriage, kinship, and gender studies. I especially wish to acknowledge the influence of Michelle Rosaldo's analysis and critique of separate domestic and public spheres in married life cross-culturally and the insights into the place of women in state societies developed in the work of Sherry Ortner. John Comaroff's perspective on marriage as a cultural process has had a profound effect on the analysis of marriage cross-culturally, including my own work in China's Canton (Pearl River) Delta.

I also wish to acknowledge the theoretical contributions made by both David Schneider and Annette Weiner to the understanding of the dynamics of marriage in societies with matrilineal kinship. The work of Arthur Wolf and Margery Wolf has provided equal insight into the domestic processes that shape marriage and the relationship of spouses in patrilineal societies. I also gratefully acknowledge Sylvia Yanagisako's contribution to the present work, in particular her analytical insight into the ways that kinship and gender practices support each other in marriage and society. I especially wish to acknowledge the influence in the present work of Jane Collier's theoretical contributions to the understanding of marriage and inequality in classless societies. The imprint of these many contributions is apparent in my own work.

Thanks are due to my editors at Harcourt College Publishers, including Bryan Leake, acquisitions editor for anthropology and sociology; Lynn McGarvin, developmental editor; and Elaine Hellmund, project manager, for their continuing enthusiasm and expert advice through the many stages of this work. I would also like to thank the many persons who read and provided helpful comments on the various drafts of this manuscript, including especially June Macklin, Evelyn Blackwood, John Shepherd, Judith Brown, Nancy Levine, James Hamill, and Donna Budani. Members of my family not only provided me with support and encouragement during the writing process but made their own expert contributions to the book: Elizabeth Stockard, Nathan Stockard, Sally Stockard Ashton, and Clark Stockard.

I gratefully acknowledge the several photographers (and archives) from whom I obtained the images that greatly enhance this book. At Documentary Educational Resources, Cynthia Close, executive director, and Karma Foley, associate producer, were extremely helpful in the selection of images from the ethnographically rich archive of the Marshall Family Collection. Photographer Thomas L. Kelly's stunning images of the Nyinba of Nepal also greatly enrich this book, and I thank him for his help in the selection and documentation of photographs from his portfolio. I am pleased to include William Fenton's historical images of Iroquois in New York; I thank him and the curator of the American Philosophical Library, Robert Cox, for assisting me in locating the photographs used in this book. I also thank Valery Garrett, Heather Shanks, James Warfield, and Patricia Wynne for providing me with their photographs and illustrations for use in this book. And I gratefully acknowledge the cartographic skills of Manuel Lizarralde, who developed the maps for this book.

There are many whose very enthusiasm for the project inspired me through the eventful period of writing. In addition to those already mentioned, I thank Candace Howes, G. William Skinner, Kristin Harrison, Ann Metcalf, Christopher Steiner, Lin Marshall, Ray McDermott, Ellen Oxfeld, Rubie Watson, and James Watson. And last, but not least, I thank my former students, especially Steve Bustamante, Sarah Ono, Timothy Reuter, Lara Bagby, Sailesh Tiwari, Michael Brennan, Zach Nathan, and Katie Zorena, for their support of their professor and her project.

For his encouragement of me, through all phases of development and writing, I especially thank George Dearborn Spindler, to whom I dedicate this book.

Janice E. Stockard
New London, Connecticut

1

Marriage as a
Cultural Practice

This book provides a unique focus on the diverse marriage practices among four societies: the !Kung San, Chinese, Iroquois, and Tibetans. As an anthropologist, my point of view emanates from a holistic understanding of culture itself. Such a context provides insight into the meaning of marriage customs as well as other social practices.

As an anthropologist conducting fieldwork on marriage and economy in South China, I sought out elderly Cantonese women as research subjects, or cultural "informants," as anthropologists call them. From the beginning, I was struck by the bewildering array of behaviors relating to marriage recounted by my informants. Some of these seemed merely rebellious, whereas others appeared to undermine marriage (as Westerners know it) altogether. They told of wives who lived apart from their husbands, most for at least 3 years, but some for 10 years or more. They related how girls swore vows of chastity to one another, declaring their intention to remain unmarried and even threatening to run away, all to escape the marriages arranged for them by their parents. How was I, as a cultural outsider, to understand these behaviors? What, indeed, was the practice of marriage here, the behavior expected of husbands and wives by the term *marriage?* What did marriage mean for spouses in this part of Chinese society?[1]

In this book, I do not analyze marriage as a strictly private domain of life, determined solely by an intimate relationship and separate from the public arenas of social, economic, and political life. Rather, marriage engages and is mutually defined

1

in relationship to these other arenas. The chapters that follow employ a distinctive theoretical perspective placing marriage within the broader context of cultural institutions, practices, and ideologies.

This anthropological perspective uses as its base the conviction that one can understand the meaning of any custom or practice only from within the complete context of the culture in which it occurs. The holistic approach to the study of culture—indeed the *concept* of culture—developed in the early decades of the twentieth century with the emergence of the discipline of anthropology itself.[2] Prior to this, both popular and professional interpretations of the differences observed in people's lives and institutions in other societies were based on conjecture and prejudice, reflecting a lack of scientific data, common ethnocentric bias, and a partial perspective on culture.

One can best describe the anthropological perspective on culture as a product of its distinctive method. The *ethnographic method,* the hallmark of anthropology, is based on extensive fieldwork during which the anthropologist lives with the people who are the subject of study, often for years. Fieldwork requires intensive preparation, including a lengthy period devoted to researching the culture and learning the language of the people who will be studied. This prefield cultural immersion creates one of the fundamental strengths of the ethnographic tradition. In the field, anthropologists can build a life for themselves among the people they study. They establish rapport, make friends, and even acquire "families," all the while engaging as fully as possible in the everyday activities and events of the people among whom they live.[3]

From this privileged position, the anthropologist, as a partial insider in the society under study, observes people in the context of their own culture. In addition to this *participant observation,* the defining method of fieldwork, the anthropologist draws on a repertoire of other methods to enhance the quality and increase the quantity of field data collected. By conducting interviews and life histories, filming rituals and recording stories, and sharing meals and just "shooting the breeze," the anthropologist tries to understand the meaning of life within another culture as the people themselves experience it. In a sense, the anthropologist engages in ongoing conversations with cultural insiders in order to share in their interpretation of their own culture and later to translate it as *ethnography,* a written cultural description that retains the original meaning as closely as possible.

For the anthropologist, therefore, marriage is best understood within the context of all other facets of culture, including polity and economy, kinship and marriage, and religion and ideology. From the anthropologist's perspective, these features together provide the cultural context for understanding the practice and meaning of marriage. In short, marriage can be understood only as a product of a specific culture, within a particular history and environment. The meaning of marriage is culturally constructed from the many distinctive values, practices, and institutions that shape every society. I present the four societies here for the diverse ways in which they organize the practice of marriage and culturally construct its meaning.

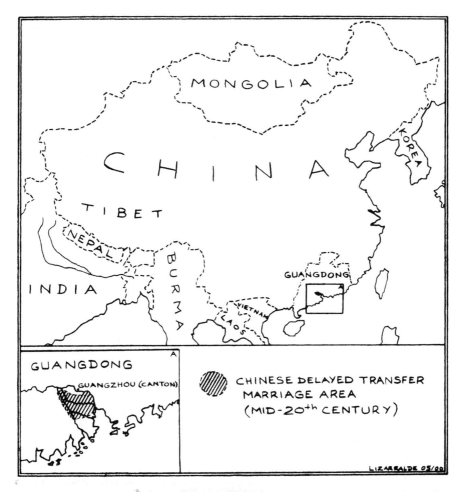

Map 1.1. South China, showing area in which delayed transfer marriage was traditionally practiced, late nineteenth and early twentieth centuries.

A SOUTH CHINA ILLUSTRATION

In my own fieldwork on marriage, I interviewed elderly women whose native villages were located in one specific area in the hinterlands of Canton (Guangzhou), at the heart of the thriving silk district of South China. This area was known throughout China for its unorthodox marriage practices and for the skill of its women (daughters and young wives) in reeling silk thread from the cocoons spun by silkworms, which most local families laboriously raised and tended.[4] During almost three years of field research, I conducted interviews, collected life histories, and listened to personal accounts of marriage and silk work from more than 150 women. They told me about their own marital experiences and working lives, as well as those of their mothers and grandmothers.

The holistic perspective on culture combined with the ethnographic method enables anthropologists to perceive—and then describe—the behaviors and actions of people in other cultures more as the people themselves understand and experience them. In my fieldwork, the challenge was to establish a more complete cultural context for understanding the puzzling (and to Chinese from outside this area, even shocking) accounts of marriage and resistance to marriage related by my women informants.[5] Over many months of fieldwork, I discovered a marriage system that was integrally linked to the local economy of the silk district. To understand the practice and meaning of marriage in this part of China, I had to first understand fully how the lives of men and women, husbands and wives, were structured by both marriage and sericulture (silk production).

Each new informant and interview provided me with the opportunity not simply to learn one more informant's experience of marriage, work, and family life but to acquire a little more of the cultural insider's knowledge. As a result, with each successive interview I learned how to ask better questions, that is, more culturally informed (sensitive) questions, of the next informant. The ethnographic method, because it is based on extensive fieldwork, creates the unique opportunity to retool interview questions continually, based on the anthropologist's growing understanding of people's own lived experience.[6] It yields rich cultural insights, providing a window into the meaning of marriage and other cultural practices.

In my research project, retooling questions across months of interviews enabled me finally to approach an insider's point of view with regard to all the informant reports of girls seeming to resist marriage and wives appearing to refuse to live with husbands.[7] I came at last to understand the dynamics of a marriage system that defied what members of American society readily assume to be an essential feature of marriage—the cohabitation of husband and wife. For the people in this part of Chinese society, marriage required by custom that husbands and wives live apart for the first few years of marriage. In my ethnography *Daughters of the Canton Delta*, I have called this custom "delayed transfer marriage":

> In the delayed transfer form of marriage, brides separated from their husbands on the third day after marriage and returned home to live with their natal families. By custom, brides were expected to live apart from their husbands for the first three years of marriage. During this initial period of "natolocal" residence, a bride was expected to visit her husband's family on the occasion of two or three festivals or family celebrations each year. The postmarital separation of husbands and wives was expected behavior and was described by informants as a "custom," like a rule or regulation. All women marrying as first wives, whether from rich or from poor families, married with delayed transfer.
>
> In delayed transfer marriages, the length of time that the spouses lived apart was to some extent influenced by individual circumstances, but informants reported that in most villages a separation of at least three years was

expected. Since the age at marriage for women in the delayed transfer area was 17 to 20, most brides were 20 or older when they finally settled in their husband's family home. The most auspicious occasion for the entry of the bride as a resident spouse was a first pregnancy occurring about three years after marriage. Pregnancy always brought to a close the natolocal stage of marriage.[8]

Thus, within this area, marriage by custom meant that husbands and wives would continue to live with their own natal families for at least the first three years of marriage, and all marriages were arranged by parents, the bride and groom meeting for the first time on their wedding day. The back-and-forth of conjugal visits enabled the new couple to become better acquainted before actually beginning to cohabit, always in the home of the husband and his parents, together with his brothers, their wives, and children, as well as his unmarried sisters. During the early years apart, young wives, resident at home, continued to work, reeling silk for their own family.

Developments in the technology of silk reeling in the late nineteenth century increased both a reeler's efficiency and the quality of silk she produced, enhancing her contributions and status within her natal family. With mechanization and the rise of silk-reeling factories offering lucrative wages, a young wife still living at home and reeling was encouraged by her family to work a little longer, stay a few more years—thereby lengthening the period of time before taking up permanent residence with her husband and his family. In families living in the vicinity of these reeling factories, young wives not uncommonly lived apart from their husbands for six years and even longer.[9] Although I did not expect this finding, I soon realized that this seemingly aberrant delay was actually customary, profoundly shaping the experience of marriage and its meaning for husband and wife.

CREATING A GENDERED PERSPECTIVE ON MARRIAGE: THE EFFECTS OF KINSHIP AND RESIDENCE PRACTICES

In recent decades, gendered analyses have yielded insight into the differing meanings of marriage for spouses, as well as for family members (beyond the conjugal couple themselves) who can be considered additional partners in a marriage. In "traditional" societies, these copartners are themselves a part of the critical context for understanding the marriage experience of the conjugal couple.[10] Thus a gendered analysis takes the meaning of marriage as culturally constructed, in part by the participation and presence of others, including the husband's parents and brothers or the wife's parents and sisters. These copartners may or may not be residing with the married couple, but they are key cultural variables, shaping the everyday experience of marriage for husbands and wives, as well as the conjugal relationship itself.[11]

A gendered analysis of marriage in traditional societies thus highlights the significant role of kinship—*who* constitutes family—in generating the different

Figure 1.1. South China silk reelers at their basins, early twentieth century.

meanings of marriage for spouses. For the reader, kinship may be an unanticipated factor in the shaping of marital experience and meaning. However, kinship clearly emerges as a dominant cultural force in creating the very different positions occupied by husbands and wives in !Kung San, Chinese, Iroquois, and Tibetan marriages. Indeed, contemporary cultural anthropologists consider kinship to be a key constituent of gender relations cross-culturally. Thus, the four ethnographic cases I discuss here show that kinship plays an integral role in shaping the different social positions and behavior expected of the genders in marriage, that is, of "husband" and "wife."[12]

In my analyses, I also highlight the role of postmarital residence practice, that is, where and with whom the new conjugal couple resides after marriage. It could be with his parents or hers—or somewhere else. Postmarital residence practice is another powerful social process, shaping the differing experiences of the genders in marriage cross-culturally. My theoretical emphasis on residence practice and its effects on gender and the marriage experience arises from my field research on Chinese delayed transfer marriage. In South China, the effects of this different postmarital residence practice (different from the normative one for most of Chinese society) on the position of daughters, brides, and the conjugal relationship itself were striking. Delayed transfer, with its back-and-forth pattern of visitation between the new bride and the groom and his family enhanced the position of daughter and bride within her natal family and reduced the hierarchy of husband over wife when she eventually settled with him after a few years of marriage. Elsewhere in China, the customary residence practice differed greatly, with distinct effects on the position of husband and wife within both their natal families and the conjugal relationship. In most parts of China, the bride settled with her husband and his family immediately after the marriage rites were performed. That very different resident practice had profound repercussions for all, which is discussed in chapter 3. Still yet another postmarital residence practice shapes the experience of marriage in the United States.

Although marriage practices in the United States are as diverse as its many different cultural traditions, the country's dominant political, economic, and other ideological systems also render similarities. One of the most invisible factors shaping marriage in the United States, as elsewhere, is postmarital residence practice. That such residence feels so natural exposes its cultural roots; in all societies, people grow up learning the right and natural way to do everything. That is what people in cultures do. In every society, across the generations and from family to family, parents work to socialize their children, which is another way of saying they give them culture, teaching them the behavior appropriate to their sex and station in life.[13]

In the United States, the postmarital residence practice assumed by a newly married couple is typically a house or apartment, rented or bought, that establishes them as a new nuclear family in the making, independent of the natal family of either the bride or groom. The cultural assumption, except within some ethnic communities, is that it is natural that nuclear families separate with the marriage of their children in each generation; the place of the new conjugal couple is apart from any established family or set of relatives.[14] This custom is called *neolocal* residence, a practice not found in most traditional societies.

In combination with other cultural practices, including the specific understanding of what and who constitutes a family (i.e., kinship ideology), the practice of postmarital residence in each society creates a different meaning of marriage for the conjugal couple, their children, and their parents as well. In most traditional societies, marriage was defined in part by the residence required of the new couple after the wedding, typically with either the bride's or groom's parents, in their house and under their authority, alongside other brothers and sisters and their spouses and children. This situation created an experience and meaning of marriage that contrasts sharply with that found in the United States.

Marriages were not just about bride and groom and their desire to marry on the basis of personal feelings, including love. Marriage served the best interests of larger family and kinship groups, including extended families and households, lineages, and clans, and was based on the economic and political interests of those larger entities. It follows then that married couples were not independent, nor was either spouse considered an "individual" who could act independently of these groups.

Residence practice, then, especially in combination with kinship ideology, is a powerful force in human society, providing not only the context for marriage but its very meaning as well. As the following ethnographic cases show, residence practice in traditional societies created in large part what it meant to be a husband or wife.

OF MARRIAGE AND THEORY

For the following analyses of the marriage systems of the !Kung San, Chinese, Iroquois, and Tibetans, I have drawn on a repertoire of explanatory frameworks that have shaped the field of American cultural anthropology. Among the relationships between marriage and other facets of culture brought into focus by the anthropologist's holistic perspective, the relationship between marriage and economy has provided many rich insights into the meaning of marriage cross-culturally.[15] My analysis of marriage bears the influence of the related traditions of American economic and ecological anthropology. Important questions deriving from these traditions include the following: How does the environment itself influence the development and organization of human society? How do material culture and technology shape and constrain human social practices, including kinship, marriage, residence, and gender? I examine the relationship of a society's technology and subsistence adaptation (hunting and gathering, horticulture, or plow agriculture) to its social organization (band, tribe, or state society) and attempt to discover the relationships among these variables and marriage practices.[16]

For example, among the !Kung San ("Bushmen") of southern Africa, I examine the relationships among hunting, the requirements of social life in a band, and the practice and meaning of marriage. In the Chinese case, the technology and division of labor characterizing agrarian life—and especially the role of the plow in generating economic class distinctions—are important for understanding the arrangement of marriage in that state society. Similarly, for the historical Iroquois, horticulture, their primary subsistence strategy (which was the province of women exclusively) proves an important part of the cultural context for understanding the conduct of marriage in that tribal society. Finally, among the Tibetans, I consider the constraints of making a living from alpine agriculture in shaping the customary marriage practice whereby a set of brothers marries one wife to share among them. In these examples, one also sees an application of neo-Marxist anthropology. Each highlights the relationship between the infrastructure (a people's material resources and the technology available to exploit them) as it influences social structure.[17]

Another theoretical influence in my analysis derives from structuralism as practiced by British social anthropologists. My focus on kinship in each society highlights the significance of descent ideology and structure—the clan, lineage, and descent line—for understanding the practice and meaning of marriage.[18] Questions explored here that bear the imprint of British structuralism include the following: How did the presence of matrilineages in historical Iroquois society (organized around female lines of descent) structure both the organization of households and marriage, shaping the meaning of the latter for bride, groom, and their kin? Why did the elder generation permit only marriage between bride and groom of different lineages?

In my analysis of the effect of kinship on marriage, I emphasize social processes, especially residence practices, that reproduce and sometimes modify kinship structures across the generations. In this respect, my analysis bears the imprint of practice theory, as developed by the French anthropologist Pierre Bourdieu.[19] To illustrate the application of this theoretical perspective, I take the example of an important kinship structure in traditional Chinese society, the male descent line and its continuity, which was the focus of the family. Practice theory directs attention to people's everyday behavior and actions. How do these behaviors and actions reproduce the structure and ideology of that male descent line within Chinese family and society? How does marriage as the Chinese practiced it create families in each generation that continue to focus on sons and the chain of male descendants—and not on daughters? Practice theory, then, focuses attention on how people's lived experience re-creates larger cultural structures, such as descent lines and lineages, residence practices, and marriage patterns.

I draw from these several theories selectively, using their concepts more as heuristic devices to explicate the cultural setting and processes that shape marriage. Gender theory as developed by the American anthropologists Jane Collier and Sylvia Yanagisako is the dominant theoretical influence on my analysis of marriage in this book.[20] In accordance with these theorists, I do not view any of the intellectual traditions identified as influencing this work as complete in its explanatory power.

In the theoretical model developed by Collier and Yanagisako, cultures are conceived of as systems of inequality, created by social processes, located in all domains of social life, including economy and polity, kinship and marriage, and religion and ideology. In this analysis, I posit marriage as a critical moment when social inequalities—whether between husband and wife, mother-in-law and daughter-in-law, or men and women in general—are both visible and reproduced.

My own contribution to this developing body of gender theory, based on my South China research, is to identify postmarital residence practice as another critical social process that creates differing experiences for men and women in marriage.[21] As such, postmarital residence generates inequalities, which characterize the relationships of the genders in societies everywhere. These inequalities are culturally constructed differently from those found in the United States, as the chapters that follow demonstrate.

Anthropologists have long identified postmarital residence as an important topic of study in the field of kinship and marriage. However, the traditional conceptualization of postmarital residence as the outcome of "residence rules" led to controversy over whether residence was a determining factor in the formation of families and households. Perhaps in the rough wake of debate over residence rules, residence as a field of inquiry slipped from the main agenda for anthropological research. I reconceive postmarital residence as a social process, thereby placing it at the heart of the analysis of marriage and gender.

MARRIAGE IN FOUR CULTURES:
SELECTION AND SEQUENCE

I have selected the marriage systems analyzed in the following chapters on the basis of their contrasting features, thus facilitating cross-cultural comparison. For example, one set of contrasting features relates to the age at marriage for bride and groom and the disparity in their ages. Other examples include the arrangement of marriage (matchmaker or parents?), the criteria for the arrangement of marriage (class membership or clan?), and the number of spouses in the marriage (one or more for the wife or husband?). With regard to number of spouses, for example, the !Kung San practice of monogamy can readily be contrasted with Chinese polygyny (whereby a husband has more than one wife simultaneously) and Tibetan polyandry (whereby a wife marries several husbands).

In addition to the contrast provided by marriage itself, a study of these four cultures allows the opportunity to compare and contrast the relationship of marriage in diverse economies and polities, exemplifying different kinship and residence systems, as well. For instance, marriage in a society with a polity considered relatively egalitarian with few social distinctions and without political leaders (!Kung San) can be contrasted with marriage in a partially stratified society with chiefs (Iroquois) and in highly stratified societies with fully developed political hierarchies (Chinese and Tibetan). In addition, these four societies invite comparison across economies, manifesting as they do different subsistence adaptations: hunting and gathering (!Kung San), horticulture (Iroquois), and intensive agriculture (Chinese and Tibetan).

The diverse kinship and residence systems of these four societies, and consequently, the contrasting experiences of husbands and wives in each, provide other cultural dimensions for comparative analysis. Thus, different kinship systems—the bilateral (tracing family membership through both sides of the family), patrilineal (tracing family membership and rights through father's side exclusively), and matrilineal (tracing family membership and rights through mother's side)—create the opportunity to view marriage within societies that differ in still other cultural dimensions. The kinship system of the bilateral !Kung San (with their shifting postmarital residence pattern) when set against the patrilineal kinship system of the Chinese with patrilocal residence (whereby spouses live with the husband's father's family) and polygyny, the matrilineal Iroquois who practice matrilocal residence (spouses living with wife's mother's family), and the patrilineal Tibetans, also with patrilocal residence, but with polyandry as well, readily suggests a cross-cultural comparison.

Through the analysis of these four cultures, a fifth culture emerges in which marriage presents yet another face. This marriage system, the one found in the United States, can also be characterized by its practices—age at marriage, number of spouses, arrangement of marriage, and criteria for marriage. In addition, this marriage system can be set in its cultural context and described in relationship to its country's economy, polity, kinship, residence, and family systems. Of course, citizens of the United States represent diverse cultural origins from abroad, as well as particular histories of change, accommodation, and resistance from within.

The analyses of the four diverse cultures that follow, therefore, provide the outlines of the major cultural dynamics and ideologies that shape our emerging marriage system(s). These features of marriage practices in the United States provide cultural contrasts with the !Kung San, Chinese, Iroquois, and Tibetan ethnographic cases. Throughout, an implicit question is posed: How does the practice of marriage in the United States manifest this culture's dominant ideologies and articulate with other major features of society?

2

Marriage among
the !Kung San
of Southern Africa

The groom was about sixteen and the bride was eight. It was considered to be an excellent match, as the bride was pretty and the groom was already becoming famous as a hunter.... The little girl did not want to be a bride. When we asked her how she felt about her wedding she hid her face in her hands and said that she was still a young child, too young to get married.

All in all, only the groom's family showed patience and forbearance until at last the wedding took place. One day the young man killed a duiker [antelope] and, according to custom, gave most of it to his bride's parents, thus proving that he hunted well and would provide for them and their daughter. With this the engagement was sealed. Shortly afterward the mothers of the bride and groom built a scherm *[thatched house] for the young couple, which they furnished with wood and water and enlivened with a fire, kindled by brands from their own fires. Very early the following day the bride's mother adorned the bride, washing her, hanging white bead ornaments from her hair, rubbing her clothing with red, sweet-smelling powder, a symbol to Bushmen of beauty. Then, sitting her upon one large* kaross *[an animal hide] they covered her with another and left her to spend the day motionless, waiting for evening, when the union would take place. . . .*

Because the sun brings death, no ceremony or part of any ceremony is performed when the sun is strong; but when evening came and the sun itself was dying, the groom was led to his new home by his three brothers, who

took him by the hands and pulled him there, forced him, for custom
demanded that he show reluctance. The bride, according to custom, refused
to go to her husband and had to be picked up by another little girl and car-
ried to him. In the drama of reluctance the bride struggled while the other
girl caught her. She lifted the bride and carried her on her shoulders, not
upright as a figure of triumph but wrapped in the kaross and motionless,
like a dead little animal, then put her shrouded body on the floor of the
new scherom *and left her there to lie quietly while the wedding guests*
arrived. Again according custom, the groom seemed to take no notice of
his new bride; the people in the werf paid no attention, and, in fact, all the
people went about their business in such a matter-of-fact way that an
observer would think that nothing had happened although the young peo-
ple were now married, the wedding had taken place.

Elizabeth Marshall Thomas
South West Africa (Namibia), 1958[1]

The !Kung San are people now inhabiting territories bordering the Kalahari desert, primarily in Botswana, Namibia, and Angola.[2] They are a branch of the San peoples, an indigenous people of Africa, numbering approximately fifty thousand, that once occupied a vast territory in southern Africa, including what is now the Republic of South Africa. Given the name "Bushmen" by European colonists, they call themselves the *Ju/'hoansi,* which means "the real people." Until the 1970s, when political and economic change forced an end to their traditional way of life, they were one of the several remaining contemporary populations in the world practicing hunting and gathering, also known as foraging.[3] This way of life, or subsistence adaptation, is believed to resemble the one characterizing all human populations prior to the development of agriculture about ten thousand years ago.

The !Kung San have been the focus of study by anthropologists since the early 1950s and are in print and media the most studied hunting-and-gathering people in the world.[4] They thus provide an unparalleled opportunity to understand the place and practice of marriage in a society vastly different from that found in the United States. Anthropologists believe that marriage among the world's hunters and gatherers may resemble in its chief features marriage as practiced by people for most of human history.

Elizabeth Marshall Thomas's account of marriage among the !Kung San during the 1950s, quoted at the beginning of this chapter, for the most part resembles the descriptions provided by other ethnographers: Girls were typically married very young, anywhere from age 8 to 12 on average. A new bride protested marriage in general and often her parents' choice of husband in particular. The marriage ceremony itself was, from the outsider's perspective, understated and hardly noticeable. The arrangement of marriage entailed the demonstration of hunting skill by the husband, who was expected to hunt after marriage not just for his wife but more important, for her father.

Atypical in Thomas's account is the relatively young age of the groom. New husbands were usually at least 18 to 25 years old, and sometimes as old as 30,

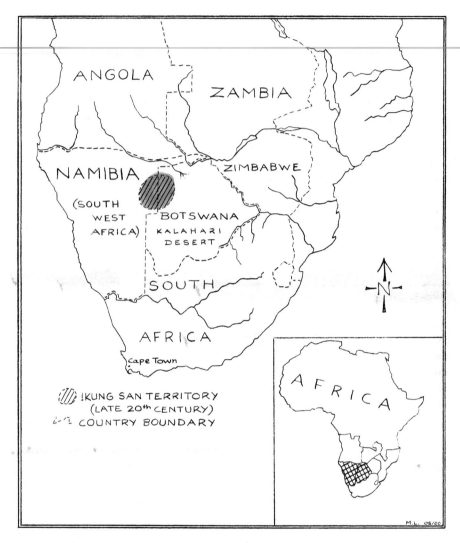

Map 2.1. Map showing primary area of !Kung San settlement, late twentieth century.

creating a disparity in the ages of the bride and groom of 10 years or more. Many if not most girls married before reaching their first menstrual period, but !Kung San feel strongly that marital sexual relations must not be assumed until the young wife is sexually mature. Indeed, they do not permit a husband, older and perhaps more anxious to begin sexual relations, to force himself on his young wife, believing it would make her crazy. Thus, marriage creates a situation in which a husband, years older than his immature wife, must work hard for her parents by hunting for them, waiting perhaps a few years before assuming a sexual relationship with his spouse.[5] What can explain this marriage practice, and what can it mean?

HUNTING AND MARRIAGE

Thomas's short ethnographic description of !Kung San marriage reveals an apparent connection between what anthropologists call a *subsistence adaptation,* in this case hunting, and the practice of marriage. In marrying, a husband assumes an obligation called *brideservice:* He must hunt for his father-in-law for many years not only to establish but also to maintain his marriage to the man's daughter.

Although most Westerners might believe marriage to be first and foremost about an intimate relationship between two people, a bride and groom, who arrange and consent to marriage of their own free will, without interference from other family members, the !Kung San think otherwise. For them and people in other societies practicing brideservice, marriage is a relationship involving more than just the conjugal couple. Anthropologist Jane Collier, who analyzes marriage in brideservice societies such as the !Kung San, identifies at least three partners to marriage, including the husband and his young wife, but most important, his father-in-law, for whom the husband must hunt.[6] With a large stake in the outcome, the parents arrange and negotiate the marriage, a matter far too important to be left to the passions and whims of the young people.

The practice of brideservice—the nature of the link between hunting and marriage—is the focus for this investigation into the meaning of marriage among the !Kung San, prior to the great changes forcing them in the 1970s to abandon permanently their traditional way of life. Marriage in a society practicing brideservice raises questions about the meaning of marriage. What can marriage mean when a bride's father is also a primary actor in marriage? What is the nature of the relationship between husband and wife?

In order to explore the link between hunting and marriage, the context for understanding not only an economy so vastly different from that in the United States but also a different political system needs to be established. As a polity, the !Kung San and other hunting-and-gathering societies are classless and characterized by only relatively small inequalities among people or groups of people. In fact, anthropologists have concluded that hunting-and-gathering societies were probably the most egalitarian of societies in human history. Traditionally, and prior to their incorporation into state societies in the contemporary era, people in these societies were not governed by formal leaders holding positions of authority in an overarching political system. They had no written laws and no formal courts or police to enforce them—in short, none of the political paraphernalia one would recognize and call "government." Instead, marriage itself was one of the primary systems of organization, functioning in a sense as politics in a classless society.[7]

THE CHALLENGE OF THE EGALITARIAN

In the anthropologist's lexicon, the term *egalitarian* describes a society with very little hierarchy or stratification, one characterized by the absence of groups enjoying political, economic, or social advantages over any other groups. In an egalitarian society, no one group exercises power over another; there is no ranking. Quite simply, all people are relatively equal. There are no specialists by occupation, no groups of people who enjoy greater privilege because of what they do or are in any way advantaged over any other group. The division of labor in the everyday lives of people in an egalitarian society and their activities and roles are primarily a matter of their age and sex.[8]

In !Kung San society, a boy of eight spends his time engaged in the same activities as all the other male children of the same age, making toy weapons, practicing hunting skills on small animals and large insects, and playing house with his female age-mates. Every mother with young children spends her days at similar tasks: caring for her children in camp and then heading out on a gathering expedition with other women—traveling perhaps a few miles while carrying her youngest child on her hip—bound for a distant grove of mongongo trees, where they will harvest the nuts that are a favorite among the people. Returning to camp, the mothers gather firewood for the home fire, over which they will prepare the evening meal for their families. Although personal skills influence the success with which people perform the tasks ascribed to them by age and sex, especially evident in young husbands' various levels of hunting ability, no social groups emerge based on these individual differences.

For anthropologists writing about persons practicing hunting and gathering and living until fairly recently in relatively egalitarian societies, the challenge is to describe a contemporary people who practice a very old subsistence adaptation. Even as the "traditional" !Kung San were observed hunting and gathering in the 1960s, their lifestyle and subsistence strategy were not relics of the past. They have never been a people "frozen in time." Over the long course of their history in southern Africa, they have adapted and changed along with their environment, and as their contact with other indigenous people increased, they practiced different modes of subsistence, such as simple farming and herding. In addition, during the past three hundred years, they have encountered and interacted with persons from the West who represent powerful state societies.[9]

OF MEN, WOMEN, AND THE DIVISION OF LABOR

The division of labor among hunters and gatherers begins at birth and is based on the determination of the sex of the child. Male children and female children are then socialized—or *enculturated*—into the activities, roles, and behavior appropriate to their sex. Through socialization over a lifetime, his or her gender, as anthropologists say, is "culturally constructed." Children become men and women whose behavior, expectations, and experiences in marriage are influenced by the cultural environment in which they grow up.

In this sexual division of labor, girls focus primarily on learning the skills required to forage as an adult married woman who will support her children and husband with the food she gathers on a daily basis. As a wife, she will make daily forays into areas where plant resources are known by species, season, and readiness for harvesting. Boys grow up practicing the skills required to hunt the large and small animals that provide meat. As future adult husbands, they will use this meat to feed their families—as well as other people.

Primarily, married women are responsible for gathering, but men and boys are not without the knowledge and skills to gather. Although gathering is not their major subsistence contribution, they must feed themselves during hunting excursions into the bush, which might require several days' absence from camp. And although men are the exclusive hunters of the highly prized large-game animals such as kudu, impala, and steenbok, women while out gathering will watch for the tracks of animals to report back to their husbands. They will also capture small animals and birds when the opportunity presents itself.

Boys grow up learning to recognize some 50 mammal species by sight, as well as their tracks, habits, and territories through all the seasons and weather conditions, although of course, these species are only a small part of the some 250 named species in their animal universe. !Kung San men are famous among other African peoples for their tracking skills. Boys learn not only to recognize the species of an animal by its tracks but to determine its sex, age, condition, and the direction in which it was headed, along with information about when and in what number it passed, all this to determine the feasibility of following it.

Crafting the weapons that comprise the !Kung San arsenal is another skill to master, particularly the bow and arrows that are among the hunter's primary weapons. The hunter must carefully apply to the arrow shaft the poison that will kill a large animal within a matter of hours. Anthropologists describe the superb tracking skills of the !Kung San hunter and the joy he takes in his tracking expertise. When a boy can demonstrate his ability to hunt, he will marry and embark, in the company of other adult men, on a few hunting expeditions each week.

Although lacking the drama and danger of hunting, the task of gathering is not simply a matter of taking advantage of casual scavenging opportunities. It also requires learning to differentiate from among some hundred different species of edible plants, about 20 of which make up most of the diet of the !Kung San people. In addition to identification skills, a girl must learn the locations, growing habits, and seasons of the trees and plants that produce the edible bulbs, fruit, roots, nuts, and gums that she will gather as a married woman. She must learn to recognize signs above ground that indicate food below in the form of roots and bulbs. She also must learn to make and skillfully use the simple digging stick to dislodge high fruit and to dig and pry roots from the ground. Later, as a married woman, she will daily gather food that will constitute the major part of her family's diet. If she is a skilled gatherer, a girl can harvest in an hour two or three thousand mongongo nuts, a highly nutritious staple that is a prized object of the gathering expedition.

Specialized equipment, including the important kaross, makes possible the long trek back to camp for a !Kung San wife, who is packing a load of nuts and carrying a young child. The kaross is an ingenious article made by men of the hide of game animals. As an article of clothing worn by a woman, it is draped and tied

Figure 2.1. !Kung San hunter demonstrating use of the bow and arrow, 1955. (Marshall Family Collection)

across her back. It can also be employed as a kind of pack, enabling her to carry a load of firewood, fashioned into a sling for her baby, or converted into a rain garment or blanket, as the need arises.

Anthropologists who have lived at length with the !Kung San and other hunter-gatherers report that, in contrast to the popular myth that "making a living" was a hard struggle for survival, people lived well—even in the Kalahari Desert—with comparatively less effort than in agrarian or industrialized societies. The !Kung San devoted only about 20 hours or two-and-a-half days each week to the work of subsistence, providing them with a varied and nutritious diet, in which meat from the hunt comprised about 30 percent of the calories consumed and gathered vegetable foods, the bulk of calories, comprised about 70 percent.[10]

BAND AND FAMILY, CAMP AND KIN

The small-scale bands into which hunting-and-gathering societies are organized consist of 10 to 30 persons. Band membership is quite flexible, and families are free to move to join family or friends living in other bands. Bands establish temporary camps in the vicinity of the plant and animal resources on which their livelihood depends. Camps therefore are not fixed settlements but are occupied only for the time that it takes to exhaust all resources, including firewood, within a several-mile

Figure 2.2. A demonstration of the use of the spear in hunting, 1955. (Marshall Family Collection)

radius. People in a band basically eat their way through the local resources, after which they relocate, carrying their few possessions, to a new site to set up camp.

Campsites are built in a distinctive arrangement in which small houses are constructed around a central open area or plaza, which is considered the common social space for all band members. Wives build the small beehive-shaped grass houses out of cut saplings that are set in the ground in a circle and bent and tied at the center to form a rounded structure, which is thatched and reinforced with horizontal branches. Typically six- to eight-feet across and six-feet tall, a house requires only a day or two to assemble, depending on the season and the protection needed. Houses are constructed so that each doorway opens onto the common social space, making domestic events public affairs. The central space is where children play and where people visit and in the evenings hold their dances.

Each house provides a family with shelter from rain and some storage space, but because the interior is small, a family typically sleeps outside, often sharing a common blanket. The family fire, kept just outside the doorway, establishes a hearth for each house. It is here that a wife prepares the food she has gathered during the day for the family's evening meal. Behind the house, ashes and refuse from the family fire are dumped. Located farther behind each house is a large cooking pit in which large cuts of meat from a successful hunt are cooked. Thus camp activities define different spatial zones that are organized concentrically and focused on the central plaza, the hub of band life.

Figure 2.3. !Kung San woman digging a root to prepare for her family's meal, 1952. (Marshall Family Collection)

The families that live together in a band, each occupying a small house, may superficially resemble the nuclear families living in their single-family dwellings in the United States. However, what appears to be a familiar family structure is formed in a distinctive way. With the establishment of a !Kung San marriage, a newly married couple assumes residence in a small house built adjacent to the house of the young bride's parents. Through the distribution of meat from a son-in-law during brideservice, the boundaries of nuclear families are regularly crossed, linking the families of the bride and groom and her parents in an important economic relationship. In addition, gifts of meat that are received by the father-in-law are shared again by him to include his daughter's family.

These patterns of distribution across households manifest a different cultural conception of marriage and family. In studying families cross-culturally, anthropologists seek to identify both family structures and the processes by which they are formed and maintained. A !Kung San society has no isolated nuclear families living apart and unto themselves in the bush—or even in camp. Each is linked in important ways to other families, as the long process of brideservice dramatically emphasizes.

Beyond the immediate families, the broader field of kinship relationships among the !Kung San also exhibits both similarities and differences in meaning with the relationships found in the United States. Although in every society relationships are created by ties of marriage, birth, and adoption, each society evaluates those ties differently. Thus, although there is the potential for people to recognize the same

20

Figure 2.4. A gatherer with harvested nuts, 1952. (Marshall Family Collection)

relationships everywhere, each society culturally selects particular relationships and creates their distinctive culturally constructed meaning. In the Chinese and Iroquois cases discussed in chapters 3 and 4, for example, relationships traced through a parent on one side of the family counted more than the same relationship on the other side of the family. For the Chinese, kinship traced through fathers was more important than through mothers, creating a person's basic social identity as belonging to father's line, not mother's. In the Iroquois case, the opposite was true, with mother's relatives figuring more significantly in the life of her children, creating for them the identity of belonging to mother's descent line. The way in which the same biological and social kinship ties are differently interpreted reflects a different cultural calculus or lens in each society.

The !Kung San practice a system of kinship similar in its general features to that in the United States, what anthropologists call *bilateral kinship*. By this system of reckoning kinship, an equal emphasis or weight is placed on both the mother's and father's sides of the family. There is no side of the family more significant than the other, no one dominant descent line or set of relatives. Children born to a marriage recognize relatives on both sides of the family as being kin.[11] It may at first seem surprising that, for all the cultural emphasis given the hunter in !Kung San society, ethnographers do not report a strong preference for male children. Instead, the birth of both sons and daughters is equally welcomed by parents and members of the band.

One difference between the !Kung San practice of bilateral kinship and that of the United States is the greater weight the former give to the sibling bond, the relationship between brothers and sisters. This emphasis is particularly manifest in the way that bands are made up of families. Families resident in a band usually have close kinship or friendship ties with others in the band. Bands are not composed of a random assortment of nuclear families but are built around a core of siblings who are descendants of the historical family attached to this land and therefore considered to be its "owners." These owned territories are each defined by a particular permanent water hole that gives them their value. Although siblings who are descendants of the original family are considered owners of the territory and water hole, this claim is not individual ownership. Brothers and sisters are owners in the sense of having a first claim. Thus, protocol requires that a band wishing to set up camp in a claimed territory first ask permission of the owners, which is as a matter of course almost always given. This core of siblings, together with their spouses and children, comprises the center of the social life of the band and invites other kin and friends to join them. Compatibility is, of course, a key consideration in such a small-scale society, dependent on close living and cooperation.

RECIPROCITY AND SOCIAL LIFE

One of the striking characteristics of foraging societies cross-culturally is what from a Western perspective seems the overly generous behavior of people—what appears to be their everyday altruistic behavior. Anthropologists living in these societies describe how everyone is regularly sharing and giving away all that they have to other people, both within the band and beyond it. The term *generosity* does not exactly describe this pattern of social interaction among hunters and gatherers because people watch each other carefully to ensure that everyone gives and shares almost everything.

The open nature of houses organized around the central plaza creates a situation whereby camp members can readily see all that others have in their possession. There are no private storage places, and nothing can be hidden away out of sight. Of course, in traditional !Kung San society, material goods are few and personal property minimal. A married couple can carry all that its family owns and walk to a new campsite, miles distant. Things people own include personal articles of clothing and ornamentation—such as prized strings of ostrich shell beads, hunting weaponry, digging sticks, dogs, trade pots, and other containers, including skin bags, knotted grass nets, and karosses.

Characteristic of life in foraging societies is a sharing ethic that extends even to what one has received as a gift, which must be shared yet again. Sharing is learned behavior, and children are taught from the earliest years that they must give away what they have. Ethnographers' accounts of camp life record regular admonishments from adults to children that they must share something with others. Adults even confront each other, insisting that they divide what they have and give the rest away. In her fieldwork among the !Kung San, Lorna Marshall recounts how she gave cowrie shells as a parting gift to every woman in the band in which she lived but on returning the following year found scarcely one shell among them. Each woman recipient had taken her necklace apart and redistributed the shells to friends and family living in other bands.[12] One of the worst charges that one person can level at another is the criticism that he or she is stingy and has held something back or is hiding something. Both adults and children will confront each other to share a little more.

This feature of social life is called *generalized reciprocity* by anthropologists, who consider it to be one of the fundamental factors in creating a relatively egalitarian quality of life in small-scale band societies. No one has more of anything than anyone else; everything must be shared. People know who has what, and they do not let anyone keep too much for themselves. This practice has a general leveling effect on people's lifestyles. Any inequality causes conflict, which everyone wants to avoid because, in a society without a formal political system or leaders with power and authority, simple conflicts can erupt into major ones.[13]

Gifts are part of !Kung San hospitality. They are the backbone of a whole lifestyle based on generalized reciprocity. People give gifts and share with others in their band. In addition, presents are offered during visits between members of different bands There is no expectation that the same type of gift or one of the same value will be offered immediately in return. Rather, a delay in the process of reciprocation in a very real sense creates a debt or obligation on the part of the recipient to return a gift at some time in the future. The person making the gift is aware of this social and material debt, which creates in that person a sense of expectation, obligation, and even security. If ever in need of something, the giver can ask the person in his or her debt. The object is not, as in capitalist societies, to repay the debt with speed and interest. The intention of the gift is rather to create a relationship on which the giver can draw in the future.

Visiting and gifting, everyday social facts among hunters and gatherers, create and sustain relationships over a lifetime and in turn create possibilities in people's lives. If, for example, a family needs to move to another band, regular gifting and sharing create alternative possibilities for joining a new band. If assistance of any sort is needed, the relationship and obligation generated by reciprocity mean that there are people who can provide the assistance required. And parents of a young man, and the youth himself, might establish a pattern of making presents of choice cuts of meat to the parents of a young girl; out of this kind of relationship, betrothals are made.

In a multitude of ways, generalized reciprocity makes social life possible. Differences among people living in a band can be leveled, reducing sources of strain and conflict in what could be described as brittle communal life. With everyone in some sense providing for everyone else, social security is built. In addition, reciprocity between people living in different bands both creates and sustains relationships across distances and thus guarantees a person support and possibility in other places.

Meat, which people in a !Kung San society especially crave, is also shared widely. Men's hunting expeditions are not as productive as the daily gathering forays of women; women provide the bulk of people's diet and most of their caloric intake. The longer a band camps at one site, the farther hunters need to travel in search of large game. In addition, hunting is characterized by a degree of unpredictability, dependent on the movement and behavior of animals in changing terrain and weather. But it is hunting prowess and the rewards that a successful hunt brings that are the stuff of !Kung San stories. People are glad when hunters return with a prized animal; they hunger for meat.

A good hunter, however, does not openly celebrate his prowess but rather enjoys a quiet kind of prestige. In this society, to assert personal success in the hunt (or at anything) is to stir up envy and create jealousy. A hunter is expected by !Kung San custom to act modestly after making a large kill, and powerful cultural processes intervene to direct his pride within socially acceptable channels. Thus, his demeanor plays down his success and makes possible the relatively egalitarian and intimate life in the band. Anthropologist Richard Lee gives the account of a !Kung San elder, who, when asked why a successful hunter makes little of his own skill and expertise in tracking and hunting a large animal he has killed, replied: "When a young man kills much meat he comes to think of himself as a chief or a big man, and he thinks of the rest of us as his servants or inferiors. We can't accept this. We refuse one who boasts, for someday his pride will make him kill somebody. So we always speak of his meat as worthless. In this way we cool his heart and make him gentle."[14]

Meat is so greatly valued that its distribution is not initially based on generalized reciprocity but is shared according to an established protocol. The hunter whose arrow is responsible for killing the animal is expected to take the best cut of meat, giving the prime piece to his wife's parents and another fine cut to his own. The men who assisted in the hunt or in carrying the carcass back to camp each also receive a good cut and in turn distribute it first to their parent-in-law and parents. Following this first order distribution, waves of further sharing follow, ending in many gifts of meat to people in the band and beyond in generalized redistribution.

The giving of meat in this society in some sense creates a kind of politics; the giver enjoys the personal prestige of having received a good cut of meat in the first place, and redistributing shares to others also creates obligation in them. Such giving is an important part of being an adult male. He is in a position as a hunter to be able to give meat and later, as a father-in-law, to receive more meat from his daughter's husband. A married woman's subsistence contributions, which are larger than a married man's, are not widely distributed in waves of sharing but feed her immediate family, her husband and children. Because the !Kung San have little means of preserving and storing food, a wife gathers only what her family needs, but if there is excess, she can choose to whom to give it.

MOBILITY AND SUBSISTENCE

Both hunting and gathering among !Kung San require mobility on the part of the provider. Neither subsistence contribution can be accomplished without travel to destinations beyond the camp, whether in pursuit of game to hunt or food to gather. Male hunting expeditions, although not mounted daily, sometimes require a few days of tracking and travel far from camp. Female gathering trips, conducted daily, also require walking great distances—in some cases several miles—and with a young child in tow and a younger one in the woman's kaross or on her hip. Anthropologists report that a wife's gathering expeditions can require 1,500 miles of walking a year.

Although child rearing is primarily women's work in this society, women are not constrained or limited in their mobility away from home by the claims of child care. Due to a prolonged period of nursing on demand that serves to postpone ovulation, women give birth to children at intervals of about every four years, enabling a mother to engage in regular gathering because she needs to carry only one child. In this society, therefore, childbirth is adapted to the requirements of a mother, who must travel widely to gather the foods her family needs.

In foraging societies, it is difficult to locate separate social spaces that define or circumscribe men's and women's lives and activities. There is no clearly defined domestic domain, for instance, where one might expect to find women exclusively.[15] (The exception perhaps being all of camp itself when men are away on an extended hunting expedition.) Typically, however, both men and women return to camp in the afternoon, where a wife prepares the foods she has gathered for the evening meal. Both parents play with the children, and a husband tends to crafting or repairing his hunting equipment.

In short, comparable personal mobility in and out of camp for both spouses is a requirement of their hunting-and-gathering way of life. Mobility is a conspicuous feature of both men's and women's lifestyles in these societies and contrasts sharply with the clear-cut spaces that emerge with the development of other subsistence adaptations. In agrarian societies like the Chinese case, for example, pronounced gendered spaces appear. With the greater hierarchy that is a characteristic feature of agrarian societies, domestic spheres emerge, defining the activities of wives and children. In almost an opposition to that space, a public sphere—beyond home and hearth—becomes the arena of politics, dominated by men.[16] Among the !Kung San, in contrast, regular physical mobility beyond home and hearth for both husbands and wives appears to be an essential ingredient to the general feeling of egalitarianism that anthropologists report, both at the level of social life and in the tenor of the relationship between husband and wife in marriage. There is an easy affection between spouses, each confident in their own important contribution to the family's well-being.

Physical mobility of several kinds is an important factor in economic, political, and social life. As already noted, the lack of material possessions makes possible the easy seasonal geographic mobility and relocation to new territories of the entire band, a basic requirement of hunting-and-gathering societies. Daily mobility in and out of camp on the part of every hunter and gatherer, husband and wife, is also a feature of the foraging lifestyle and marriage. No less significant to the quality of life in these societies is the resort to physical mobility on the part of persons to avoid, escape, or reduce interpersonal tensions between members of a band—or a marriage.

MEN, WOMEN, AND CONFLICT

In a society with no formal political leaders or institutions to administer customary law or police people's conduct, various means develop to reduce the tensions arising when people anywhere live in close proximity and interdependence. From prodding people to share in order to reduce the inequality that surfaces when anyone has more meat or ostrich shell beads than someone else to forcing people to talk out their grievances rather than nursing them in growing resentment, all are social measures that serve to level out difference and alleviate sources of conflict. Unshared or hoarded anything provokes others to insist on a share—or causes fighting.

Anthropologists studying hunting-and-gathering societies have observed that the two primary sources of major conflicts are meat and sex. Therefore, cultural protocols to regulate access to both are developed. In the case of meat, the !Kung San carefully adhere to the protocol for distribution, and all members of the band watch to ensure it is done properly. The organized waves of sharing reflect concerns about the equitable parceling out of a precious commodity and reduce tensions and conflict within the band. With sex, as well, betrothal and marriage are cultural means of organizing or regulating sexual relations that serve to limit, for instance, open competition by adult men over claims to one woman.

The !Kung San believe that unmarried women cause conflicts, perceiving that fewer women are available for marriage than men seeking wives. Every girl marries because remaining single would provoke rivalry and fighting. This may be one explanation for the engagement of girls at such a young age. They become engaged to older husbands who establish a claim to a particular girl as wife by arranging to perform brideservice for her father. In a sense, brideservice as a cultural practice regulates access to both meat and brides through a relationship established between the bride's father and husband. Brideservice is the continuing claim a husband stakes in the parents' daughter as his wife and is an economic commitment that lasts for 10 years or the birth of three children. Anthropologists of brideservice societies— the Comanche are another example—report that husbands work hard at brideservice and talk about it all the time.[17] One meaning of this marriage practice is that it is a public demonstration of a husband's continuing claim that he makes to establish this wife as his.

Should a dispute between two people seem headed for open conflict—as in a dispute over ownership of an animal killed in the hunt and claimed by hunters of two different bands—then they resort to mediation in an attempt to calm tempers and resolve the brewing conflict. According to ethnographers, people in !Kung San society can readily recount past occasions when minor disputes escalated quickly to anger, lost tempers, and the resort to the poisoned arrows that people grow up learning to respect—and fear. At these moments of mounting crisis, people turn to what can be called the "informal leaders" in these societies, men or women (usually men) who are respected for their judgment and renowned for their skill in facilitating the talking out of differences.

The reputation as informal leader is established on the basis of several criteria, including membership and seniority in the set of core siblings, the reputed owners of the band's territory. These qualifications are reinforced by the support and confidence of the people of the band and the person's demonstrated ability to make the peace by forcing the disputants to talk out their difference. Informal leadership among the !Kung San, can be observed in the general "political" discussions, open to all members, concerning matters affecting the welfare of the entire band. Women actively participate in these discussions, but men do most of the talking.

From a cross-cultural perspective, the engagement of women in politics—if not quite equally, then at least actively—is notable. Some scholars believe that this participation by women as almost the equal counterparts of men is based in part on the physical mobility they experience in their everyday lives. Mobility gives them the information about the band's subsistence situation and about the concerns of neighboring bands and other indigenous peoples that are the stuff of political discussion. Mobility both through gathering and through visiting and gifting—which is a form of politics—enables women to contribute to broad-based political discussion. In addition, mobility substantially enhances the security and lifestyle of the wife's family. Mobility creates, in essence, political life for both husbands and wives.

Mobility is also key to the final resolution of a conflict that proves too stubborn for even the skilled mediation efforts of an informal leader. As fighting seems all but inevitable, people will physically take hold of disputants to separate them; they maintain physical contact to try to control and defuse the situation and allow tempers to cool. If intervention fails and resolution seems unlikely—and fighting has not erupted—one disputant and his family may leave the band and join another. Continuing confrontations are too large a risk for the entire group, and once mediation fails and time does not heal the conflict, everyone agrees that the outcome must be physical separation and the relocation of one party to another band.

Family and kin ties and friendship, nourished and sustained by regular visiting and sharing over the years, thus in the end creates a multiplicity of possibilities for a person who wants to join another band. Indeed, anthropologists of the !Kung San have observed that band membership is flexible and that people frequently establish a new home in another band. Thus generalized reciprocity across bands creates alternative residential groups.

TO EARN A WIFE:
PASSAGE TO MANHOOD AND BRIDESERVICE

Traditionally in the !Kung San, marriage is a relationship among a husband and wife and the wife's father and is at the outset firmly based on compatibility between the two men. A father-in-law will depend on his daughter's husband to hunt well and to provide him with the regular choice portions of meat that are the basis for brideservice. A new son-in-law will need to depend on his father-in-law and his wife's brothers to learn the territory in which he now lives. He will also depend on both his mother-in-law and father-in-law to help manage their young daughter, his bride; for all that marriage means in the early years, a young girl may resist and rebuff him. If the marriage succeeds, a son-in-law will be resident in the band of his wife's parents for many years.

With so much resting on the choice of husband, neither the selection of a candidate nor an evaluation of his hunting ability and personal qualities is left to chance—or to the desires of a young girl-bride. Marriage, in particular first marriages, are not then primarily about a relationship between the bride and groom, based on sexual attraction and love. With such a stake in the outcome, parents arrange the first marriages of their children.

A young man must demonstrate a certain level of hunting expertise because he will support his father-in-law in brideservice. A man who cannot hunt will not be given a wife. To be considered eligible for marriage, then, a young man must undergo what in effect is a rite of passage, publicly marking his transition from the world of boys and unmarried youth to the world of adult men. Adult men are eligible to marry, and marriage in turn gives a man an active role to play in the everyday social and political life of the band.

The adult married men of the young man's family and band conduct the initiation. The rite occurs on two separate occasions, each marking his mastery of hunting. He is required to hunt and kill two large herd animals—such as duikers (antelopes); one must be male and the other female. After each kill, the men gather to celebrate the further passage of the young hunter from mere youth—who are called "people of the shade"—to adult man. On each occasion, he is scarified on a different side of his body, including his forehead, arm, and chest, by one of the men, who uses a sharp blade. After the cuts are made, one by one, a specially prepared fatty paste is rubbed into the small wounds.[18]

On completion of both stages of the rite of passage, a young man has publicly demonstrated his hunting prowess, making the transition to a man who is eligible to marry. Hunting in the life of youth is therefore immensely significant; on completion of the ritual, he will want to marry—because every young man needs a wife to live the full life of an adult man in !Kung San society.

Parents scout the field of eligible bachelors for a suitable husband for their daughter, who may at the beginning of their search be a very young girl. Because there is much visiting among bands and relatives reside in other bands, parents can easily learn of the best prospective candidates. They are anxious to find the right husband for their daughter because of their continuing stake in her marriage. Although hunting prowess is an important quality, so are reputation and personal qualities. In a society in which an angry or hostile young man can cause problems for everyone, provoking conflict and fighting, parents look to find a husband with the qualities !Kung San admire.

Once the right candidate is found and the marriage takes place, *uxorilocal* residence is assumed, whereby the new husband comes to live in his wife's band. This residence practice obviously facilitates the young husband's fulfillment of his obligation to hunt for his in-laws in brideservice. In a sense, brideservice establishes marriage as a process, not a single event. As a public demonstration of his continuing claim in their daughter, the process of brideservice symbolizes his marriage to the daughter of his parents-in-law. Should he cease hunting for them, his claim ends—as does his marriage. But no husband wants to return to the unprivileged life of a single man.

Although !Kung San girls are married relatively young to older husbands in arranged marriages, this situation does not render a girl powerless. As young as she is, and with no choice but to marry, a young bride does have a voice in the ultimate selection of a husband. Grooms by all reports eagerly take up the obligations of marriage, whereas brides routinely object—and sometimes fiercely resist. She can through her protests object to their choice, and if efforts to reconcile her to the marriage fail, he will be sent away. Most of all, a young bride objects to being married because then she is expected, even as a 10-year-old girl, to act like an adult married woman and begin the work of a wife, leaving aside the play and games that she might wish to continue. She is expected to live with a stranger and to begin "keeping house" for her husband by gathering for his meals and preparing cooked food before the hearth that she must keep.

Young girls in !Kung San society have every reason not to want to marry—it is an arranged match that abruptly ends their girlhood games and freedoms. The early years of marriage for a daughter are not infrequently a series of several trial marriages, although no husband will be lightly sent away after all the careful planning, and the obligations of brideservice, from a groom's perspective, are not to be lightly laid aside. If he is sent away, his divorce means he must assume again the status of bachelor and begin brideservice in a new marriage.

MARRIAGE, PARITY, AND POLITICS

A young man in !Kung San society is keen on assuming his place alongside the other adult men in camp, taking on the obligation of hunting for a father-in-law in order to claim the privileges of marriage. As a husband, he will have a wife to provide him with many things. She will build him a house around the central plaza in camp and keep a hearth fire, over which she will cook meals from the food she gathers for him daily. In order to become fully adult with a place in camp and a voice in the political life of the band, that is, become a social equal with other adult men in this egalitarian society, a man needs a wife. In a sense, a wife establishes him as an adult, creating parity between him and all the other adult men in camp.[19] Marriage therefore is an achievement for which he works hard in brideservice. Here, then, is a very distinct meaning of marriage in !Kung San society.

As a married man with a place in camp, the groom will enter fully into the discussions and activities of political life in camp. His opinions will be heard, his advice sought. He can be a host to guests, family, and friends visiting from other bands. If he and his wife have daughters, he will eventually have sons-in-law to hunt for him and provide him with more meat. The brideservice of sons-in-law will allow him in turn to be able to give meat away in generalized reciprocity, enhancing his position in society.

Parents' eagerness to acquire a husband for their daughter, therefore, is not just about eating better; it also provides them with meat to distribute to fellow band members and to friends and relatives in different bands, which is the basis of social life, security, and possibility. Even as he grows old, the father can continue to extend hospitality, visit others, and gift his visitors and hosts with shares of meat he has received from his daughters' husbands. Given the full context of social life among the !Kung San, a married man has achieved all the possibilities of a full life. There are no corporations to run, armies to lead, bank accounts to fill. A married man is at the apex of the male adult world—alongside all the other adult men in camp.

The position of married men, with a place in camp and society, can be contrasted with the lives of young men prior to marriage. Unmarried young men have no real role in political life but exist on the margins of camp life. No one takes them very seriously. They cannot be real adults because they have no house of their own, no fire, and no daily cooked meals. With no regular place in camp, they can only ask for things from others, including cooked food from their mother, who is

Figure 2.5. !Kung San bride and groom with wedding party in front of the new house constructed for the occasion, 1952. The bride sits on the left side of the entrance to the house. The bridegroom, who now begins his term of brideservice for his father-in-law, sits on the right side of the entrance. (Marshall Family Collection)

anxious to see them married. People in general see them as potential troublemakers for married men's wives. As bachelors who have passed their initiation rite, they are only casual hunters, for they do not yet have a father-in-law for whom to hunt in brideservice, no wife to claim through public demonstrations of hunting prowess. Anthropologists have been surprised by the apparent lack of hunting drive among bachelors, beyond establishing their eligibility to marry in the rite of passage. Bachelors are truly the "people of the shade," with no marriage, wife, or father-in-law.

Prior to their bachelor years, boys play together practicing their hunting skills on handy targets, including small animals such as porcupines and even anthills. Girls play together engaging in running and ball games. Boys and girls also play together

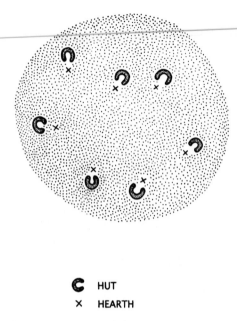

C HUT

× HEARTH

Figure 2.6. Diagram of a typical campsite, showing the arrangement of open-sided houses around a central social plaza.

in imitation of adult life, playing house and a game called "getting married," a game primarily initiated by the boys. Thus every !Kung San child has engaged in some measure of sexual experimentation and comes to know in the intimate life lived in the camp just what a husband and wife do under the common blanket they share with their youngest child.[20]

Parents of children engaged in this game of marriage are aware that their children are not just building playhouses but playing at sex, too. Adults discourage the game within view of camp, sending them out of sight into the bush, but they do not try to stop it. The generally relaxed parental attitude toward premarital sexual play and experimentation is a striking feature of !Kung San childhood, especially when contrasted to the more supervised play in the United States, where children are discouraged from too early sexual knowledge and from experimentation. Among the !Kung San, however, this activity occurs within the context of the intimate social life within a band and camp.

Anthropologists have observed that the boys are more keen to initiate the game of "getting married" than are the girls. A girl probably already has a good sense of what marriage means for her in the not-too-distant future, when she will be engaged and married to a man perhaps 10 or more years her senior. The disparity in ages at which girls and boys marry creates a situation in which boys about the age of 10 find that their sexual playmates are deserting them one by one, becoming the wives of adult husbands. With no wife of their own for several years yet, these youth may to a certain extent earn their reputation by trying to seek the attentions of married women. At precisely the same moment that a young girl objects to the marriage and husband arranged for her, and the new work both create, her husband leaves the marginality of bachelorhood, accepts the wife chosen for him, and eagerly takes up the work of brideservice. At the outset, therefore, girls and boys have differing attitudes toward marriage, reflecting the different meaning marriage has for each.

RESIDENCE AND THE RELATIVELY EGALITARIAN LIFE

Marriage among the !Kung San cannot be described as being established on egalitarian terms. Although the marriage is an arranged one for both bride and groom, and each is a stranger to the other, the differences in their ages—within the context of the meaning of marriage for each—differently conditions them to marriage. She claims she is too young for the world and work of the adult married woman; he readily assumes a hunting obligation to her father in order to claim her as wife. It is not so much the girl in particular he is claiming as much as a wife in general, who will bring him everything a man in the world of the !Kung San could want. Yet the girl-bride is able sometimes to convince her parents to send a particular husband away. How can the persuasive power an extremely reluctant child bride exerts on her parents be understood?

One of the notable features of marriage in !Kung San society is that, just when marriage begins to seem not so egalitarian, a new bride's objections can prevail. Yes, she must marry, but determined resistance to one husband and objections beyond the mere fact of marriage will win her parents' ear. They will send the first husband away, even though he may have worked months at brideservice, and find another husband for her. She must marry, but they will heed her persistent protests. The influence such a young daughter can wield on this occasion is remarkable from a cross-cultural perspective. Daughters in most agrarian societies, which are highly stratified (such as traditional China), could protest their arranged marriages, but their cries would not change parents' plans for the marriage.

One of the key factors in understanding the young bride's influence in the !Kung San is the early extended period of uxorilocal residence—the new couple's residence alongside her parents' in their band. She is a bride, but due to uxorilocal residence, she remains to some extent still the child of her parents. She continues to grow up under the guidance and still-watchful eyes of her parents, who remain her guardians. Therefore, her complaints are heard. Her parents can protect her from any husband who, because of his greater age, experience, and strength, turns abusive. They can even decide to terminate the marriage. Parents are also able to ensure that their young daughter is her husband's only wife. Although a few men in !Kung San society (less than 5 percent) take an additional wife, parents feel that this situation is not in a daughter's best interests because rivalry and fighting can result. Thus, through uxorilocal residence, parents can guarantee in a number of ways the best possible beginning for the marriage of their young daughter to her older husband.

Uxorilocal residence lasts for the full period of brideservice, 10 years or the birth of three children. After that, the long-married couple, socially now a stable one, can move to join a band of their choice, sometimes choosing to join the husband's family's band, which is called *virilocal* residence by anthropologists. Thus the !Kung San can be said to have practiced an early uxorilocal postmarital residence practice, later often followed by a shift to virilocal residence.

The different ways in which something almost invisible to an outsider—a residence practice—can temper the relationship between spouses is perhaps one of the most underappreciated cultural factors shaping marriage. In all societies in which one spouse or the other by custom moves to live with the other and his or her parents, the effect is to isolate the one who moves from the ready support of the natal family. Postmarital residence practice can therefore serve to either weaken or empower one spouse's position in the new marriage. The Chinese case (chapter 3), in which young brides move to join their husband's family, provides a dramatic contrast to the effects of early years spent in uxorilocal residence in !Kung San marriages.

Following perhaps an early period characterized by one or more trial marriages, a young !Kung San bride eventually settles down with a husband. After a period of several years and the birth of several children, the marriage becomes more equitable and more emotionally satisfying for both. Anthropologists observing hunting-and-gathering societies find that surviving the first five years or producing several children are good indicators that a marriage may be long-lived. Long marriages are not uncommon.

As already noted, the early years of marriage may be characterized by trial marriage and divorce. Divorce in this society is relatively easily accomplished, compared with divorce in class societies with property invested in marriage. Domestic fights are frequently the consequence of discovering that a spouse has been conducting an extramarital affair. Fighting over sex, as noted previously, is one of the primary causes of conflict.[21] Typically, open conflict, arguing, and sometimes physical fighting precede divorce between !Kung San spouses. However, cultural factors usually intervene to prevent injury in domestic fights. These fights occur in camp, where the rest of the band can see and hear everything. As in all disputes that threaten to escalate, other band members will intercede, separating the spouses, to prevent real harm from occurring. Because divorce itself is accomplished by the departure of one spouse from the band—the remedy for all unresolvable conflict—everyone prefers divorce after a certain level of regular conflict has been reached. The spouses will at some point decide to part company rather than continue fighting.

Although many spouses remain faithful, certain reasons specific to the culture may be said to predispose a wife or husband to establish a sexual relationship outside of marriage. When a marriage ends in divorce, a wife will leave her husband for a new husband and marriage; there is socially no place for an unmarried woman, unless she is elderly. Because people believe that unmarried women cause conflict and fighting, a recently divorced woman quickly remarries, often to someone she

Figure 2.7. !Kung San couple in front of their house. The husband binds an arrow to its shaft with sinew, while his wife works at her own project, 1952. (Marshall Family Collection)

knows. It is in a sense a good strategy for a wife in the early years of marriage or in a troubled marriage to line up a possible replacement for her husband in case she should need to leave her present marriage.

In the event of divorce, young children remain with their mother, and hence a divorced father will have to live apart from them. Whether the marital breakup is hostile or amicable, the husband's lifestyle suffers more than the wife's. Without a wife, he rejoins that marginal world of the bachelor, losing the spouse who enables him to assume a place alongside the other adult men in !Kung San society. He no longer enjoys parity with the other adult men in camp, he no longer has the house and hearth with meals prepared for him by a wife who gathers daily, he loses some of his status as an adult with no home from which to offer hospitality, and he becomes a potential troublemaker because he needs a wife. Thus a husband stands to lose much more than just a spouse with divorce. By contrast, a divorcing wife suffers no comparable decline in her status or lifestyle. She will always receive a share of meat in the regular distribution in camp or from a lover. She will marry again almost immediately.

Figure 2.8. Husband and wife sit with company in the typical fashion, their guests encircling them. Among the visitors are a daughter and daughter-in-law, 1952. (Marshall Family Collection)

Because of this potential diminished lifestyle, the sensible husband is at least thinking of a potential wife he could marry if his own should die or leave him. He is, by the very meaning of marriage for men in this society, almost motivated to have a lover just in case. Nonetheless, people expect spouses to be faithful to one another and do not condone adultery. When they occur, affairs are conducted discreetly; when they are discovered, they cause fighting. A wife who learns her husband is having an affair is hurt and angry. A husband who discovers his wife is unfaithful has every reason to feel threatened—and is angered over the possibility of losing his wife and what that will mean to him. A husband in this position wants to fight her lover and may strike out against his wife, too. However, a husband who tries to hurt his wife will only cause her to leave him. In effect, the very meaning of marriage—and divorce—serves to enhance the well-being of a !Kung San wife and, from a cross-cultural perspective, her relative autonomy in society.

■ ■ ■

The case of the practice and meaning of marriage in a classless society—one characterized by relatively egalitarian relations between husbands and wives—stands in sharp contrast to marriage in a class-based society such as China, discussed in chapter 3. In traditional Chinese society, economic classes were organized in a hierarchy, as were the relationships of the genders, both inside and outside marriage. One can ask certain questions about that society: What were the connections among marriage, economy, and polity? How did the Chinese practice of patrilineal kinship, in contrast to the bilateral system of the !Kung San, affect the meaning of marriage? How did their different postmarital residence practice, that is, *patrilocal,* shape the relationship of husbands and wives, as well as their differing life experiences?

3

Marriage in Traditional Chinese Society

The dowry of the bride is carried in procession through the streets with as much parade and show as the amount of the furniture will possibly admit. Not infrequently, when the parties are near neighbors, the procession of porters or bearers, instead of taking the shortest route from the residence of the bride to the residence of the groom, takes a circuitous route through the principal streets for the purpose of exhibiting the furniture. In the case of the rich, often a large amount of superior household furniture, as wardrobes, tables, chairs, trunks, coverlets or quilts, the exterior of which is silk or satin, and various less showy yet expensive articles, is thus carried in procession through the streets. The number of persons employed in transporting these things sometimes amounts to one hundred, or even more. Those who can afford the expense have some of the articles bound around or fastened to the carrying-poles with pieces of red silk, or red crape, or red cotton cloth. This is considered a great day for the families most especially concerned, and every thing connected with the procession is designed for display. . . .

This outfit is procured, in most cases, to a great extent, by means of the money which has been furnished the family of the bride by the family of the groom for that purpose. In the case of wealthy families, little dependence is actually placed on receiving money for this object, though valuable presents of money are always made to the family of the bride by the other party. The poor generally find it impossible, in marrying off a daughter, to be at much expense over and above the amount of money received from the family of their future son-in-law.

Reverend Justus Doolittle
South China, 1865[1]

In great contrast to the understated marriage ceremony among the !Kung San and other hunter-gatherers are the elaborate rituals, grand displays of marriage goods, and other pomp and circumstance of weddings in agrarian-state societies. Of all the contemporary and historical agrarian states, traditional Chinese society provides some of the richest ethnographic material on marriage practice, as well as one of the more dramatic contrasts with !Kung San marriage.[2] The weddings of the elite and the poor present another set of contrasts.

The Reverend Justus Doolittle, a long-time observer and chronicler of Chinese social life and customs, described marriage ritual among the wealthy in the province of Fujian in South China during the nineteenth century. As illustrated in the account quoted at the opening of this chapter, great exchanges of property were clearly being transacted in weddings among the upper classes; the transfer of property between the families of bride and groom included cash in one direction and a parade of household goods in the other. Embedded in Doolittle's account of the drama surrounding weddings of the elite is the observation that, for the poor, marriage was simpler.

Although the marriage ceremonies differed from the elite to the poor, it was a difference in scale and expense, not in basic form or meaning.[3] Throughout China, everyone struggled to make the best marriage for a son, as reflected both in the lavishness of the event and in the social station of the bride. Even for the poor, weddings were a major family expense, and families willingly put themselves in debt in order to emulate as closely as possible the marriages of the elite.

A large part of the cultural context for understanding marriage in traditional Chinese society relates to the society's political and economic standing as one of the world's great agrarian-state societies.[4] Chinese society was clearly not egalitarian but highly stratified, crosscut by the interests of different social classes. Varying access to economic resources, power, and prestige created a hierarchy of classes, each characterized by different lifestyles, occupations, and opportunities. A vast bureaucracy, staffed by officials and presided over by the emperor and his ministers, effectively ruled an empire of diverse peoples, some of whom were ethnically Chinese (Han), while many others were members of different ethnic groups whose lands had been taken by the Chinese. An elaborate judicial system, backed ultimately by the armed force of the state enforced a written legal code, supplemented by imperial edicts.

In traditional Chinese society, four main classes—the elite, artisan, merchant, and peasant—composed the social hierarchy. At the apex was the elite class, made up of those men and their families who were either scholar-officials or scholar-gentry, the former ranking higher in prestige and holding official position in the state bureaucracy. Both scholar-officials and scholar-gentry were landed, leisured, and literate. They had vast agricultural holdings, land that they themselves did not work, depending instead on the hired labor of poor peasants. Because they and their families were wealthy, they were freed from domestic labors, employing great numbers of staff to clean, cook, and see to the smooth running of their households.

Members of the elite class dressed in silk robes embellished with panels of fine embroidery. Elite males had the luxury to pursue the prestigious path to academic degrees, qualifying them for high administrative posts with great financial rewards. Because the state based its official appointments on success in several tiers of state civil service examinations, degree aspirants needed decades of rigorous schooling in the Chinese classics to attain the most prestigious and lucrative positions in the empire. The elite lived extravagant lifestyles, entertained lavishly, and engaged in expensive hobbies, such as collecting art, books, and antiques.

The lifestyle of poor peasants stood in stark contrast. In Chinese society, as in other agrarian-state societies, the peasant class comprised approximately 80 percent of the population. The Chinese considered farming a respectable occupation and held the peasant class in higher esteem than the artisan and merchant classes, which they ranked ideologically below it. The label *peasant* covers a broad range of rural inhabitants who owned and farmed their own or other's land to varying degrees. Some people owned land and could afford to hire others to farm all of it for them. Others owned some land and although they could afford to hire seasonal labor, still needed to work some of the land themselves. Some families cultivated all the land they owned but needed to send some sons out into other occupations because their sparse holdings could not support all family members. The poorest peasants owned no land at all and lived only by hiring themselves out as itinerant laborers, working the fields owned by others.

The lifestyle of a poor peasant who owned even a little land was still difficult. He perhaps owned a small plot at one end of the village and another smaller piece in a hilly spot, farther from the river that was the source of irrigation waters. Daily life was a ceaseless struggle to eke out a living from the land, coaxing a crop of rice from the river parcel and perhaps beans from the other, enough to eat and still sell some to sustain the family. Land, in essence, was the basis for the great disparity in lifestyles. From the life of privilege and indulgence led by the scholar-official to the struggle of the poor peasant, inequality and hierarchy characterized Chinese and other agrarian-state societies.[5]

Marriage practice also reflected this hierarchy. Weddings were not characterized by a modest, barely perceptible ceremony, simple change of residence, and social recognition. In China, marriage united not just individuals and nuclear families but also extended family networks in particular class positions. Marriages entailed strategies to unite families in such a way as to maintain or advance these positions in society. Especially among the elite, marriages could create valuable social and political alliances across families and larger kinship units.

Contributing to the rise of the state with its hierarchy of classes was a subsistence adaptation very different from that of the !Kung San. The Chinese and all other agrarian-state societies were founded on a specific mode of agriculture based on the plow. Land was the subsistence base for Chinese plow agriculture, just as, in a different way, it was for !Kung San hunting and gathering. Among foragers, people used land as a resource base across which they moved in small-scale bands, harvesting the animal and plant resources with the seasons. With plow agriculture, however, people invested resources in the land itself, improving both land and crop productivity with intensive irrigation and fertilization.[6] Therefore, land ownership becomes significant. With this system of agriculture (which contrasts with the simpler system of horticulture practiced by the Iroquois, discussed in chapter 4), high crop yields could support much larger populations, settled at permanent sites, than could either foraging or horticultural regimes. The high-calorie grains, such as rice and millet, which were the preferred crop of plow agriculturists, could be readily stored and enabled the rise of great cities and states, dependent on large populations engaged in farming.

OF HUSBANDS AND PLOWS

Agrarian societies as a type shared cultural features that shaped the practice and meaning of marriage. The introduction in these societies of the plow as the instrument of cultivation (in place of the hoes and digging sticks that comprised the technological inventory in horticultural societies) influenced the relationship of husband and wife as well. One of the more notable characteristics shared by all agrarian societies is the cultural dominance assumed by males in plow agriculture itself. This dominance carried over into kinship, marriage, and residence practices, as well as in the processes shaping family and household. These hierarchical relationships replaced the more equitable relationships that were possible within horticultural societies.

Across agrarian cultures of various historical eras, plow agriculture favored the labor of men. Men behind the plows cultivated the fields on which these societies were based. Anthropologists have advanced various theories to explain this shift from a varied division of labor between husbands and wives in horticultural societies. Some put forward the strength theory, which attributes men's monopoly of plowing to the on-average greater upper-body strength of adult men over women. According to this theory, the physical advantage favors males for the heavy labor of plowing the field, which often required the simultaneous management of large draft animals, such as the water buffalo used in South China. Other anthropologists favor the expendability theory, based on the growing need to physically defend agricultural land from outsiders. Land brought under cultivation, and into which much labor and many resources were invested, was highly prized. Perhaps defense of land by fathers and husbands engaged in farming fields outside settlements best enhanced the possibility that future generations would survive back at home, in the protected homesteads occupied by wives and children.[7]

Accompanying the introduction of the plow was the shift to new varieties of crops, the most important in China being wheat, millet, and rice. In contrast to many of the crops grown by horticulturists—such as root crops—grains provide a

Figure 3.1. Chinese farmers behind the plow without benefit of ox or water buffalo, circa 1900.

more-concentrated source of calories that can be stored for extended periods.[8] However, grains require additional labor in processing to prepare them for storage and cooking. This task has been assumed cross-culturally primarily by women. Whether the new dominance assumed by fathers and husbands in agriculture was due more to defense and survival needs or to the greater predisposition of males for plowing and females for grain processing may never be definitively determined, as the historical evidence may be elusive.

Men's rising dominance in agriculture created further implications for marriage and the relationship of husbands and wives. Anthropologists have discovered that women's overall participation in farming and their contribution to subsistence declined with the introduction of the plow. In horticultural societies, husbands and wives divided the labor of cultivation, a particular division of tasks characterizing each society. In some, women as mothers and wives assumed a small role in cultivation, whereas in others, as among the Iroquois, mothers and their daughters assumed all the tasks of cultivation. In the Iroquois example, men's only agricultural task was the initial clearing of the land of trees, large rocks, and brush cover—an important role in cultivation, but only one of several.[9]

Another discovery found cross-culturally is that women's participation in public and political life diminished with the rise of plow agriculture. The question arises whether this change relates to men's increasing role in affairs of defense and cultivation in agrarian societies. Both activities are located beyond the home where, anthropologists theorize, men engaged in this work regularly came into contact with other groups and societies, different languages and customs, and as a consequence were better placed and therefore "qualified" to lead in political matters.[10]

To this complex mix of important changes that occurred in human societies with the advent of plow agriculture, still another must be added. Anthropologists have found that, with the rise of agrarian societies, a more rigid division of social space between men and women emerged than characterized hunting-and-gathering societies and many horticultural societies. A domestic sphere, shaping and defining the lives of wives and children, became defined in contrast to a social space beyond the household, that is, a public sphere defined by the activities and interests of fathers and husbands. In agrarian societies, the two gendered spheres are not equal, activities and actors in the public sphere being more highly esteemed and rewarded than those in the domestic one.[11] The emergence of ranked domestic and public spheres in agrarian-state societies is in turn reflected in the hierarchy apparent in the marriages and families in these societies.

MALE DESCENT LINES AND MARRIAGE

The hierarchy characteristic of society at large in traditional China was mirrored in family life. The relationship between husband and wife in Chinese marriages was an unequal one. A wife was subordinate to her husband, whom she was obligated to serve and to whom she owed respect. The leading moral philosophy of Chinese society, which guided both conduct in government and at home in the family, promoted this inequality. By the tenets of Confucianism, proper hierarchy was modeled in the relationships that were known as the "three bonds": between ruler and subject, father and son, and husband and wife. Each knew his or her right place in the hierarchy, as well as the conduct expected in that position. Within the home, these family values were found in the everyday behavior of a man toward his wife and children, and theirs toward him.

Developments in Confucianism came to definitively prescribe that a woman's proper place in society was inside the home or family compound, not outside it. The hierarchy that by definition characterized the right relationship between a husband and wife was manifest in their everyday behavior toward one another and was explicitly taught to their children as family values. The binding of women's feet in constricting cloths, footbinding, became more pronounced in the degree to which the natural foot was deformed, especially among the elite class. In that class, families could afford to demonstrate that none of their wives and daughters were required to perform hard field labor—their bound feet would not support them. Wives could effectively be constrained in the privileged domestic space of upper-class households, with its hierarchy of servants, by the crippling effect of this practice.[12]

Confucian teaching certainly exerted a profound influence over the Chinese family and its dynamics. But other powerful cultural forces were also at work establishing the inequality of spouses in marriage. On entering a family home of any social class in traditional China, a visitor would first encounter the family's domestic ancestor altar, situated in a prominent place of honor in the main entry hall. On that altar, wooden tablets were arranged in a hierarchy of generations and genders, each representing the deceased members of the family. The family regularly burned incense and made ritual offerings at this home altar to honor and sustain the deceased in the life beyond. This practice of paying respect to the ancestors as an obligation of the living to the deceased, who they believed still had power to work influence in the lives of their descendants, is what is called in the West "ancestor worship," in particular, male ancestor worship.

Although ancestor tablets could also be erected to represent a deceased mother or son's wife—especially if recently deceased—the deceased male members of the family provided the focus and continuity. The male descent line was the backbone of every Chinese family, and marriage and postmarital residence practices served to continue and celebrate this line. The Chinese conceived of it as an unbroken line of descent that could be traced back to deceased men of the family, long since departed, and forward into the future—in what they hoped would be a continuous chain of male descendants, spanning the generations.[13]

One addition to the list of changes associated with the rise of agrarian societies—adding to what some see as almost a watershed or paradigm shift in human cultural history—is the shift to family systems that favor male offspring, the growing prominence of male lines of descent, and marriages built to support all of these things. Men, after all, were fathers, sons, and husbands behind the plow.

Patrilineal kinship in traditional Chinese society was a powerful influence on marriage practice and was one of the key factors shaping the meaning of marriage for husbands, their wives, and families. Some anthropologists and other scholars of Chinese society consider this ethnographic case as perhaps the most extreme example of a patrilineal society because of the particular power of the male descent line. All agrarian societies were essentially patrilineal in orientation. Nonetheless, the supporting practice of male ancestor worship in the Chinese case gave the dominance of the male line additional force. Although it is important in all patrilineal societies for a father to have at least one son to carry on his name, to support him in old age, and to inherit his property, male ancestor worship in traditional Chinese society created a religious obligation to continue the father's line of descent. It was a moral duty of the highest order to have a son, to assure that the line of your grandfather and father—your line—continued unbroken through the generations.

This moral duty gave marriage in Chinese society its primary goal: to produce sons to continue the descent line of the husband. As manifest in virtually every aspect of marriage and residence practice, as well as in the relations of husband and wife to one another and to other members of the husband's family, the meaning of marriage was clearly tied to the demands of the male descent line. The cultural norm and ideal form of marriage throughout most of Chinese society was what has been called the "major" form of marriage. It was the occasion for the great transactions in property described by the Reverend Justus Doolittle.

With property, reputation, and descent lines at stake, the arrangement of marriage was, as for the !Kung San, not left to the bride and groom. Parents controlled the selection of spouse and arranged the marriage between a bride and groom who

Figure 3.2. Interior view of a Chinese ancestor hall, South China. Tablets honoring deceased male ancestors of the lineage are arranged on the altar.

had never met. Major marriages were thus by design both arranged and "blind," the spouses seeing each other for the first time on the actual wedding day. In stratified societies such as agrarian states, the control over the selection of spouse and the arrangement of marriage served to support the continuation of proper hierarchy within the family. Cross-culturally, marriages based on attraction between bride and groom—love matches—jeopardized the control exerted by senior members of the family over juniors. Where a postmarital residence practice creates an extended family situation by adding the newly married couple to an already-established family and household, a marriage based on love threatens the authority of parents over the adult married children of the family. In the Chinese case, major marriage required the bride to assume residence with her husband and his family in what anthropologists call patrilocal residence.

By definition, the betrothed were strangers to one another so that the married son's loyalty and obedience to his parents would not be undermined by his new wife. If the marriage were based on love, a new wife might too easily encourage her husband to shirk his filial duties in his attentions to her interests. Not only were marriages, then, not founded on love, but parents discouraged any outward signs of affection between their son and his wife for similar reasons. A compatible and loving relationship might grow out of an arranged marriage, but the public display of affection between husband and wife was not viewed by his parents as being in the best interests of the family.

45

TO ARRANGE A MARRIAGE

To arrange a marriage, parents engaged the services of a matchmaker, whose business it was to know the sons and daughters available for marriage in a number of villages situated within one rural market district or urban neighborhood. In a major marriage—which was the norm, as well as the cultural ideal in most parts of China—both spouses were married as young adults, the bride usually several years younger and sometimes still in her early teens. For the matchmaker, one basic consideration in surveying the population of unmarried young adults was to establish who was eligible to marry whom, based on the greater kinship identities of bride and groom.

In traditional Chinese society, the male descent line around which a family was built could be traced back across the generations to one distant male ancestor. If that ancestor had several sons, then his own direct line of descent would diverge into the several lines of his sons. If each fulfilled their filial obligation to produce sons to continue the direct line of their own common father, those sons produced descendants that then divided the direct line of their father into several branches, and so on. Over many generations, all males who shared descent from the original or "focal" ancestor became a vast pool of descendants, some deceased and some living, who shared a genealogy and surname and a common lineage or clan identity. If the living male descendants organized themselves into what was in essence a corporation based on their descent line, then they comprised a what is called a lineage. (The lineage incorporated on the basis of land put in trust by its members and held as a group investment.) If the descendants were dispersed with no common collective interests, they claimed only the same clan identity. In either case, the basic marker of same lineage or same clan membership was a shared surname.[14]

In Chinese society, marriage between a man and woman sharing the same surname—the outward sign of kinship identity—was forbidden in law and in custom and considered incestuous. A bride inherited her father's surname and thus his lineage and clan identity, although she did not officially belong to either. Therefore, a matchmaker had to survey the field for candidates of different kinship identities. Her task was made more challenging when working in a market district in which entire villages were inhabited by men of one lineage. In the case of the large lineage villages characteristic of South China, for example, the two or three thousand men living in one village might all belong to the same lineage. In this situation, none of the daughters of any of these men were eligible to marry any of their sons. Thus, the business of matchmaking entailed sorting information gathered from a number of local villages to propose an appropriate marriage to the parents of the young people.

In suggesting possible matches, a matchmaker put forward the names of young people from families with good standing in the community. The personal reputations of the individual candidates for marriage were also carefully scrutinized, but only the bride's reputation could include no hint of scandal because she must be a virgin. A young woman whose virginity was thought to be compromised was certainly unmarriageable. Because there was no place for an unmarried daughter within

Chinese families, a daughter tainted by scandal could only turn for a livelihood to prostitution in one of the larger towns.

Another goal in arranging a major marriage was to match up brides and grooms of similar class standing. Through marriage, both families sought to promote their own best interests, strategizing to create a marriage that would bring them economic or political advantage. As the field of prospective marriage candidates narrowed, a further hurdle to the advancing negotiations loomed. The personal horoscopes of bride and groom had to be matched in a process undertaken to ascertain that there would be no obstacle to the marriage. After that began the hard negotiations over the amount and content of the wealth to be exchanged by the families of the betrothed.

The business of reaching agreement on bridewealth and dowry, essential to the successful conclusion of marriage discussions, was a delicate negotiation involving not only fortune but social "face" as well. Bridewealth and dowry were fundamental features of the major form of marriage. Through the exchange of property a relationship was established beyond the narrow conjugal one between bride and groom. Marriage linked families, embedded in particular positions in the class hierarchy and society. Thus, the fathers in both families worked hard to reach agreement on the wealth that each was to exchange, creating the most advantageous family connection. The groom's family paid a large sum of cash, the bridewealth, to the bride's family.

As Doolittle correctly observed, the bride's family typically used the bridewealth to offset the expense of assembling the dowry. In some cases, the dowry might exceed the bridewealth, especially if the bride's family wished to publicly exhibit its high social station. Dowry consisted of the many household effects that a new couple would need to furnish their new quarters in the husband's family's home. At marriage, the bride took with her to the groom's home all the items agreed upon during the long marriage negotiations, including furniture, quilts, curtains for the bed, tea sets, cookware, and jewelry—everything in the quantity and quality specified. The dowry was paraded through the streets from the bride's home to the groom's, announced along the way by musicians, and closely observed by the gathering crowds, a public display uniting two families in marriage. Should a new bride arrive for her wedding with a dowry deficient in items agreed upon, she would be severely abused and harshly treated in her new home—and sometimes returned to her family, ruining any chance of future marriage prospects.

The bride arrived at the groom's family home on the wedding day transported in a curtained red sedan chair—red being the color of joy. The bride and groom saw each other for the first time when he lifted the red veil covering her face. Such an important occasion in the life and future of a family was celebrated with feasting and festivities to the extent the husband's family could afford, and even beyond. For the groom's family, the solemn rites of marriage performed before the feasting commenced perfectly symbolized the meaning of marriage. Both bride and groom knelt down, bowing their heads several times to the ground before the domestic altar on which were displayed the husband's ancestor tablets.

Figure 3.3. Bride in traditional headdress, South China, nineteenth century. (John Stuart Thomson)

BRIDES AND LINES

The goal of major marriage, reflected in the marriage rites, was clearly to continue the groom's male descent line. From the groom's family's point of view, the expense and long months of planning were an investment that would eventually yield the desired grandchild, the family's male heir. From the perspective of the bride's parents, their daughter had married as well as they could afford and now had left them to live with her new husband and his family in patrilocal residence. Although it was good to know she was married—she could not have stayed unmarried and continued to live at home—Chinese families considered the expense of the dowry to be a burden, even though the bride-wealth payment may have exceeded what was in the end paid out for the goods needed for her dowry. Her family's calculation that their daughter was fundamentally goods on which one loses was based on factoring in the expense of raising her. After all, from the moment of birth, her parents knew

Figure 3.4. Groom, South China, nineteenth century. (John Stuart Thomson)

that their daughter must inevitably leave them at marriage. Conventional wisdom was that raising a daughter was like watering another man's garden.

The meaning of marriage for a daughter was then inextricably linked to her position via male descent lines. Unlike sons, daughters were born outside their father's male descent line and never incorporated as members. At best, daughters could be described as having a temporary attachment or affiliation to their father's line, being in effect temporary members of their father's family and household, and everybody saw them as more like relatives, not family members. They were born outsiders who therefore stood unable to continue their father's line by providing it with sons. It was a condition of being female that daughters must marry and move to join the family of her husband.[15]

In South China, a noteworthy aberration existed in the rich silk-producing districts around Canton (Guangzhou). There, in the early twentieth century, teenage girls began to enjoy the opportunity of lucrative employment in the local silk factories. These jobs benefited their own natal families, and daughters working in silk factories were highly prized at home. When their marriages were eventually arranged, they were in the singular position for married women throughout all of Chinese society to negotiate a delay in patrilocal residence, in order to continue working, as described in chapter 1.[16]

Despite achieving independent financial security, these women did not remain single and living in their parents' home, but all married. In their explanations as to why they didn't choose to continue to stay at home and work in the silk factories rather than marry, what can be called a "daughter's perspective" on the meaning of marriage in Chinese society became apparent. On marrying, a daughter gained an attachment or affiliation to her husband's descent line, which in turn established that she could die in her husband's home—an important consideration. Without marriage and the attachment to a husband's line that it brought, a woman was trouble for her natal family; women could not remain unmarried without bringing harm to their own family. Because a daughter was not a member of her own father's descent line, she was not allowed to die in his house. Without an attachment or affiliation to his line, which defined the family, her spirit would become at death a hungry, menacing ghost, capable of causing havoc to her own family, including sickness, death, infertility, and even crop failure. An unmarried daughter was such a threat to the fortunes of her natal family that, even if she became severely ill, she was removed from her father's house and taken to an outside shed, as a precaution against dying and haunting her father's house.

If a daughter did die before marriage, and therefore before an affiliation to a husband's descent line had been established, she would not receive a proper ancestor tablet as would a deceased son. His would be made of wood and installed on the family domestic altar, alongside the tablets of other deceased males of her father's line. A deceased unmarried daughter received only a small paper tablet placed on the floor, near the door. Then, after her spirit reached appropriate age, a marriage was arranged for her to the spirit of a deceased man, in essence, a spirit groom. A spirit marriage, too, required the services of a matchmaker. With a marriage accomplished, the spirit of a deceased unmarried daughter then had a proper place in the afterlife. A posthumous marriage was still considered marriage, providing her with the needed tie to a male descent line and spiritual security after death.[17]

These realities constitute a meaning of marriage that is specific to the experience of a woman born in Chinese patrilineal society. In a sense, a woman married for the sake of her very soul. Although a woman gained a husband and children who could provide economic security and emotional fulfillment, elderly women I interviewed stated that, even if marriage (and fate) brought a girl a blind or lame or disfigured husband, she still needed marriage for the spiritual security—the "host" in the afterlife that it provided.[18] Why was spiritual security of such concern? The reason lies in the very nature of patrilineal kinship in this society, which was believed to extend beyond this life into the next, to include both the male ancestors as well as future sons of unborn generations. Descent was traced through males during life as well as in the next life. Everyone needed to belong to a line in both lives. For females, marriage, not birth, provided this affiliation.

Figure 3.5. Sedan chair and bearers convey bride to her husband's village and home.

The requirement that daughters at marriage move with patrilocal residence was a powerful cultural force shaping the experience of being a daughter, wife, and mother in Chinese society. Residence was key in shaping the experience of males as well, marked first by the joyful reception given to a newborn son, reflecting his position in the family and line. Although he too had to marry, as a husband he would not leave his parents but remain at home to support them in their old age. He was a permanent member of his parents' family and home.

THE WIFE IN THE HOUSE THAT MARRIAGE BUILT

Following the marriage rites, festivities, and a brief visit home three days after marriage, a new wife would settle uncomfortably into the family life and home of her husband—uncomfortable because her husband was a total stranger to her, as were all the others of his family with whom she would remain for the rest of her life. Although her husband had also married a stranger, he was at home after marriage, already established in the family. The bride was alone, with no family readily at hand to support her through the transition to wife and daughter-in-law. Indeed, a bride traditionally married into a family living in an entirely different village than hers. Her contact with her own family was from then on minimal, perhaps consisting of an infrequent visit or brief reunion at a wedding or funeral.

The new wife had to learn her role and responsibilities on the lowest rung of the family hierarchy. She joined a household composed of her father-in-law and mother-in-law, their married sons and daughters-in-law, unmarried sons and daughters, and grandchildren. It was a family and household focused on her husband's line of descent. All eyes were on the new wife, who was not, perhaps contrary to modern expectations, spoiled and indulged by her status as recent bride. She was expected to accomplish her purpose as a wife: to produce a male child for her husband. Her lot as the newest member of the family meant that, until then, she would be the one worked hardest by her mother-in-law, who supervised her in her daily chores. The mother-in-law held supreme authority over her in the established hierarchy of family members and traditionally assigned the new daughter-in-law much of the household drudge work. The new wife's position in the household and domestic hierarchy improved only with the birth of her first son.

The relationship between the mother-in-law and her perhaps several daughters-in-law has traditionally been characterized by the Chinese as full of conflict. Indeed, opinion traditionally held that women were the troublemakers in the family, even rivals. Daughters-in-law fought among themselves, too, causing their husbands (who were brothers) to quarrel, which was not in the best interests of family harmony. This difficult relationship among the women of the family, who shared common origins as "stranger" wives and yet seemed to find little basis for cooperation within their husbands' family, can best be understood as a consequence of the family structure. The customary patrilocal residence practice shaped to a great extent dynamics within the family.

The Chinese case provides perhaps one of the clearest examples of the power of residence in reinforcing the position of one spouse over the other, empowering the permanent resident (the husband, in this case) and isolating the newcomer (the wife) in a house focused on an exclusive line of descent. Through the regular practice of patrilocal residence across the generations, a family sent daughters off in marriage to the villages and households of their new husbands—in effect dispersing the family females while retaining the males. Not only were daughters dispersed; they became members of households in which their interests were pitted against those of the other in-marrying wives, generation by generation.[19]

Each new wife set about trying to establish for herself both a place and security in her new life. The strategies she typically employed were to create a close relationship with her husband—who could defend her interests and support her in the family—and to produce the family's desired grandson. With the birth of children, each wife—in response to her position as always somewhat of a stranger in the family—sought to create strong emotional bonds of love and loyalty in her children, especially her sons.

The structure of the household, with all daughters-in-law under the authority of their mother-in-law and sharing in one household budget, created competition and rivalry among the daughters-in-law. Each sought to protect the best interests of her own children and carefully watched whose children received better treatment, clothing, or food. In seeking to defend her own children's interests, a wife typically sought to turn her husband against his brothers. Each wife thought that her own

Figure 3.6. Line drawing of a South China village.

family—what anthropologist Margery Wolf calls the *uterine family,* composed of a woman's children—would fare better if the household were to divide.[20] With division and separation, her husband and his brothers inherited equally from the family estate, giving her own children a more secure future, she believed. A wife quietly pressed for an early division of the family and estate, before the death of her father-in-law, the typical occasion for division.

Each wife's primary objective was to carve out a separate and secure situation for her sons, who were her future. This goal conflicted with the plan of her mother-in-law, who sought to preserve the unity of her own adult sons—who were her own uterine family. Wives as outsiders marrying into families structured in this way could only be perceived as a source of conflict in the family.

POLYGYNY: MORE AS BETTER

Further complicating the dynamics of the relationship of a wife in her husband's family and household occurred when her husband married an additional wife, creating a polygynous marriage. Marrying another wife was expensive, but men of the elite class could afford it and were motivated to both marry and enjoy less permanent alliances as well. If a first wife did not produce a son, a wealthy man would certainly seek to marry again in hopes of producing the important male heir. Men of this economic and social station might also decide to marry again just for pleasure. An additional wife (or several) was a luxury and a mark of elite-class standing. Because none of the wives were expected to contribute to the domestic economy, multiple marriages became a kind of conspicuous consumption.

A husband's additional wives were ranked in the order in which they married into the family, thus perpetuating proper family hierarchy. Each received her own separate quarters. The position of a junior wife could, however, be enhanced in the event she produced the only male children. Her status in this case would advance

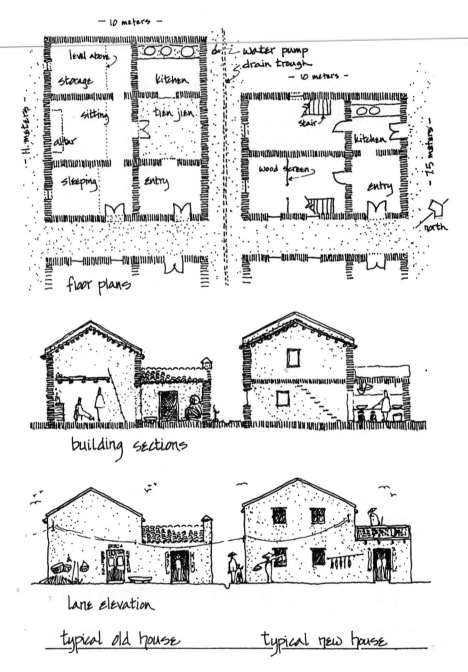

Figure 3.7. Traditional and contemporary house design, South China. Note the altar for the family's ancestor tablets in the main sitting room of the traditional house.

Figure 3.8. Generations: Doting grandparents in rural contemporary South China, and ...

Figure 3.9. ...their son and grandson. (James P. Warfield)

at the expense of the first wife's, inevitably creating rivalry and jealousy. There was thus very little basis for cooperation among cowives in Chinese society, as each strove to carve out her own uterine family. If people believed one wife caused problems in the family, the addition of more certainly confirmed this.

Although wives in polygynous marriages were ranked, they were all technically "wives," whose children were recognized as their father's. All sons born of wives, primary and secondary, inherited equally from their father's estate, although older sons enjoyed a slightly higher status by virtue of their age. There is debate among scholars over the status of additional wives in traditional Chinese society.[21] Calling them simply concubines or prostitutes may serve only to confuse matters; although men of the elite class could keep the former and visit the latter, they were not wives. However, it was also permitted to have additional wives who married into the family with patrilocal residence, bowing before their new husband's male family ancestors.

These secondary wives did not marry in exactly the same fashion as the primary wife for these marriages were not major marriages. A man chose his additional wives himself, employing the services of a go-between to arrange the transfer. Most significant, a secondary wife generally came from a family of lower economic and social standing than the first wife, and one that could not protest their daughter's lesser position in the husband's family.

In South China, the source of many secondary wives was the vast pool of domestic servants. As young girls, they were sold by their impoverished parents into domestic service in elite families, who used them as maidservants. The lifestyle of every well-to-do family required the services of a full hierarchy of domestic staff. When a maidservant reached the age of about 16, her employer was expected to marry her off. If attractive, she might be chosen to marry into a wealthy family as a man's secondary wife. In this case, instead of the transfer of bridewealth from husband's family to wife's family and the return of dowry from the bride's to the husband's, only a simple payment was made. The husband, through a matchmaker, made a payment to the employer, who technically owned the maidservant.

This one-way transaction in effect represented an outright purchase of a young woman from her employer. With no family to support her with dowry, by necessity she made a less-prestigious marriage into her husband's family than had the primary wife. Her secondary position in the family added complexity to the established hierarchy of wives already in place. The case of a secondary marriage makes clear the significance of dowry in a primary, major marriage in creating a place for a wife in her husband's home. In a secondary marriage, a wife suffered reduced status in her husband's home because she arrived without the dowry that materially and symbolically established her as a wife with proper family credentials.

■ ■ ■

In the case of historical Iroquois society, marriage created a much more modest hierarchy between husbands and wives than in traditional Chinese society. In an apparent mirror image of the Chinese practice of patrilineal kinship and patrilocal postmarital residence, the Iroquois organized both kinship and residence around women, related through the female line of descent. Such differences give rise to a variety of questions: How did this contrasting system of relationships affect the practice of marriage and its differing meanings for husbands and wives? What was the relationship between marriage and the practice of horticulture among the Iroquois? What was the connection between farming and postmarital residence practice in this society, and how did this connection influence the relationship of spouses?

4

Marriage among the Historical Iroquois

Marriage was not founded upon the affections.... When the mother considered her son of a suitable age for a marriage, she looked about her for a maiden, whom, from report, or acquaintance, she judged would accord with him in disposition and temperament. A negotiation between the mothers ensued, and a conclusion was speedily reached.... Not the least singular feature of the transaction, was the entire ignorance in which the parties remained of the pending negotiation; the first intimation they received being the announcement of their marriage, without, perhaps, ever having known or seen each other. Remonstrance or objection on their part was never attempted; they received each other as the gift of their parents. As obedience to them in all their requirements was inculcated as a paramount duty, and disobedience was followed by disownment, the operative force of custom, in addition to these motives, was sufficient to secure acquiescence....

When the fact of marriage had been communicated to the parties, a simple ceremonial completed the transaction. On the day following the announcement, the maiden was conducted by her mother, accompanied by a few family friends, to the home of her intended husband. She carried in her hand a few cakes of unleavened corn bread, which she presented on entering the house, to her mother-in-law, as an earnest of her usefulness and of her skill in the domestic arts. After receiving it, the mother of the young warrior returned a present of venison, or other fruit of the chase, to the mother of the bride, as an earnest of his ability to provide for his

Map 4.1. Map showing area of Iroquois settlement, seventeenth century.

household. This exchange of presents ratified and concluded the contract, which bound the new pair together in the marriage relation.

Lewis Henry Morgan
New York, 1851[1]

The marriage ceremony among the historical Iroquois was modest, and marital life began with the simple movement of the groom to the bride's home, the longhouse. There, the new husband assumed residence with his new wife, alongside others of her extended family, but one organized differently than in the Chinese case. Residents of the Iroquois longhouse included family and relatives of the bride's mother, who belonged to her female descent line. Thus, the potential field of family and relatives who might be living in the longhouse at any one time included the bride's sisters and unmarried brothers, their mother and her sisters, as well as the daughters

59

and unmarried sons of those sisters and possibly the maternal grandmother. The spouses of the female family members would also be co-resident in what was, in fact, an elongated dwelling, divided into individual compartments in which component families lived. The focus of the longhouse was a line of descent, but one traced through females, not males as in the Chinese case. The matrilineal Iroquois with their matrilocal residence practice provide what appears at first to be a mirror image of patrilineal, patrilocal Chinese culture.

Societies with matrilineal kinship comprise only about 15 percent of the world's cultures.[2] Most of these matrilineal societies are based on the subsistence adaptation of horticulture, simple farming employing hoes and digging sticks, but not the plow. Matrilineal systems are rarely found in agrarian societies or pastoral societies. Neither are they characteristic of industrial or postindustrial societies.

Societies practicing horticulture displayed great variation in their kinship systems. In some, families, lineages, and clans were based on male descent lines, in others on female descent lines. Still others were bilineal—in which some important rights and statuses were inherited through the male line, and others through the female line. Still other horticultural societies placed no emphasis on either descent line.

The kinship systems found in horticultural society assumed slightly different meanings, varying from society to society, created in part by the different postmarital residence practices that occurred in each. In horticultural societies, greater variation in these residence practices was found cross-culturally than in societies based on any other subsistence adaptation. Shaped by differing postmarital residence and kinship systems, horticultural societies displayed a remarkable array of marriage practices and meanings.

This diversity in kinship, residence, and marriage arrangements that characterizes horticultural societies is found in conjunction with partial stratification, called *rank*. Unlike foraging societies, social groups develop in horticultural societies that can be ranked by their differential access to prestige. The polity in these societies is characterized by the emergence of systems of ranking and formal political hierarchy and authority. However, each ethnographic case is tempered by a distinctive combination of kinship and residence practice. Although Iroquois society is a rank society—there are male chiefs—this in combination with the cultural emphasis on matrilineal descent and matrilocal residence created in the Iroquois society an interesting balance between male and female.[3] Traditional Iroquois society had an almost egalitarian feel reflected both in marriage practice and in the relationship between husband and wife.

THE IROQUOIS IN HISTORY

Historically, the Iroquois people held dominion over important territory in the American northeast. At the peak of their political strength during the seventeenth century, they held strategic lands against the claims of rival tribes through a combination of success in battle, skillful negotiation, and intimidation. Their territory, which encompassed lands situated in what is now upstate New York and Ontario, stretched along Lake Ontario and the Saint Lawrence River. After more than three hundred years of contact, first with Europeans, then with Americans, through trade, conflict, and unequal treaties, the land of the Iroquois is today much reduced. They hold title to small reservations, primarily located in New York and Ontario. The cultural life of the Iroquois has adapted to the realities of industrial and postindustrial life. In the United States, although the Iroquois nation is encapsulated now within a capitalist-state society, it has retained many important traditions, including the kinship, residence, and marriage practices that are markers of the distinctive Iroquois identity.

This exploration of Iroquois marriage practice and meaning focuses primarily on the nineteenth century and earlier. Still perhaps the best ethnographic source on the Iroquois was written in the mid–nineteenth century by Lewis Henry Morgan, a New York attorney. He began his own amateur ethnographic explorations into local Iroquois political and kinship systems, which were, he discovered, bound together as one. At the time, the United States had no formal discipline of anthropology and no practicing anthropologists. Morgan devoted years conducting fieldwork among the Seneca—one component tribe of the Iroquois confederacy—alongside his Seneca informant, Ely S. Parker. Through his conversations with Parker and visits to the reservation over a period of years, Morgan's work assumed an ethnographic quality.

Morgan discovered that the political system—his object of study—was linked to many other features of Iroquois society, including their kinship and residence systems. He published his research findings as *League of the Ho-de-no-sau-nee, or Iroquois* in 1851 and further research and comparative analysis as *Ancient Society* in 1877. His discovery that the Iroquois kinship system, built on female lines of descent, provided the basis for male political hierarchy focused the attention of Westerners on the subject and interpretation of kinship.[4]

The historical significance of Morgan's ethnographic research is immense. His published work on the Iroquois provided a major intellectual source and inspiration in the development of Karl Marx's theory of historical materialism and the basis for Friedrich Engel's *The Origin of the Family, Private Property and the State, in the Light of the Researches of Lewis H. Morgan*.[5] Morgan's writing presented to a wide audience of Americans and Europeans the first ethnographic description of life in a matrilineal society. Out of the striking contrasts between kinship as practiced in Iroquois society and in European and American societies, the field of kinship studies was born.

Following the exploration of the Chinese case, a focus on historical Iroquois society in some sense provides a cultural inversion. However, Chinese society was highly stratified and based on plow agriculture; Iroquois society was only partially stratified and based on horticulture. As a subsistence adaptation, the regime of horticulture can be characterized as simple farming, without the use of the plow, and without extensive irrigation systems or intensive fertilization. This system of cultivation provided the basis for the development of only limited hierarchy, both politically and interpersonally.

Figure 4.1. Iroquois (Seneca) young woman, nine-teenth century.

Figure 4.2. Iroquois (Seneca) young man, nineteenth century.

Figure 4.3. Iroquois (Seneca) village showing arrangement of longhouses, seventeenth century.

HORTICULTURE AND THE DIVISIONS
OF LABOR IN KINSHIP

Iroquois employed simple tools, primarily digging sticks, to prepare the soil for planting crops. The most significant crops were the "three sisters"—corn, beans, and squash—but they also cultivated the sunflower, grown for its oil and meal, as well as various leafy greens. They first had to clear the land of its forest cover to ready it for planting. This required felling and burning trees, the ash acting as simple fertilizer. A feature of the division of labor in all horticultural societies is the assignment of the task of clearing the land to men. Among the Iroquois, clearing was followed by cultivation, undertaken by women exclusively, who assumed the tasks of preparing the soil, planting, weeding, and tending the plants, as well as harvesting the mature crops.

Anthropologists theorize that the practice of horticulture may have spurred the cross-cultural development of complex systems of kinship, including the rise of large corporate kinship groups such as lineages, described previously for Chinese society.[6] Farming entails an investment of labor in the land in a way that hunting and gathering does not. Foragers stand in a different relationship to land, using the land as a base over which they travel to exploit the game and plant resources. Horticulturists use land as a basis for planned production. Labor improved the land through clearing and tending, and it could then be replanted across the seasons and years, but not indefinitely. Land became exhausted without the intensive measures employed in agrarian societies, its fertility used up in a matter of years.

How were claims to the best improved land to be apportioned? How could claims to improved land and its productivity be assigned? Kinship systems, anthropologists theorize, provided a sure means of assigning cultivation rights to persons on the basis of a fixed identity—determined by their membership in recognizable lines of descent, for instance. Large (from a nuclear-family perspective) extended kinship groups—based on descent line, lineage, and clan membership—developed in part, it is believed, to establish clear claims of "ownership" over specific parcels of land. Rights or claims by persons to farm or be supported by the products of the land were then determined either by birth into these kinship groups or by marriage into them.

In the Iroquois case, a person could claim a right to cultivate certain fields through birth into a matrilineage, a descent group founded on an unbroken line of mothers, maternal aunts, and grandmothers. Birth established membership in the mother's matrilineage, regardless of sex. Sons and daughters inherited, by virtue of their kinship identity, a right to work land belonging to their mother's lineage and to be sustained by its products.

OF LONGHOUSES AND FEMALE DESCENT LINES

Matrilineages occupied a longhouse, spilling over into several houses, depending especially on the number of daughters born to it. The possible residents of the longhouse, listed previously, should be considered a section or fragment of a matrilineage. Only daughters of the lineage, however, could pass on membership in the lineage to the next generation of children, both sons and daughters. Sons born to a matrilineage did not pass on their lineage identity directly because their own children belonged to their wife's lineage; only through one's mother did one inherit a lineage identity, conferring membership in the land-holding group. A son of the matrilineage could not biologically extend his mother's descent line or lineage; his children belonged to *their* mother's lineage.

As the exclusive cultivators of the land owned by their lineage, the women of the matrilineage co-resided in one or more longhouses, contiguous to fields held by the lineage. Women born of the lineage were the permanent residents of the longhouse, while a brother, on marriage, moved to live with his wife in her lineage longhouse, on her lineage land. For the duration of his marriage and residence, he was expected to work for her longhouse and to father children to continue her lineage into the future. His continued marriage and residence with his wife was, in a sense, contingent on fulfilling these productive and reproductive roles. All eyes in the longhouse monitored his performance.

The longhouse was an elongated dwelling, built of slabs of elm bark over a framework of long poles usually stretching about 100 feet in length, although large houses extending to 300 feet have been reported. Typically, longhouses were approximately 25 feet wide and at peak reached 23 feet high. A defining feature of the interior space was a central corridor running the entire length of the house, along which hearths with smoke holes were situated at regular intervals of about 23 feet. On both sides of the corridor were the living and sleeping spaces for the separate families, partitioned by walls into individual family compartments. Each was furnished with benches for sitting and sleeping. The two families residing across the corridor from each other shared a centrally located hearth. Longhouses typically housed about eight separate families but could be extended in length to accommodate more.

The women of the longhouse were also considered "owners" of the house and the tools needed for cultivating the fields. This property then passed on in turn to the next generation of female lineage members. Technically, property could be said to pass down through the female descent line. But as anthropologists have pointed out, property was not significant.

Tools of cultivation consisted primarily of simply crafted digging sticks that could be easily made. When worn or broken, they could be thrown away and replaced. Houses themselves periodically needed to be rebuilt as the timbers decayed. Before long, the land, too, became exhausted. In addition—and reminiscent of the shorter rhythms of !Kung San band relocation—after a period of time, the firewood collected by the Iroquois women required expeditions that took them too far from camp and were therefore unproductive. Horticulture as a mode of agriculture could not support long-term or permanent settlement like the towns and cities in agrarian societies.

For these reasons, the Iroquois needed to relocate entire villages after several years to allow exhausted fields to lie fallow and regain their fertility. Iroquois villages

Figure 4.4. Seneca women shucking corn, Allegany Reservation, New York, 1930s. (William Fenton)

were usually abandoned and rebuilt on the average of every 12 years. Thus, the Western conceptualization of ownership in terms of the legal claims of individuals must often be set aside in the case of rank societies (and in foraging societies), where ownership confers rights to use a resource rather than possess it exclusively in perpetuity.

People in Iroquois society did not have much to own in the way of personal or collective property. Hence, the interpretation of culture within a society practicing matrilineal kinship should emphasize but not overstate the right of lineage women to own, control, and pass on property to their daughters. Remarkable from a cross-cultural perspective is the daughter's natural ability, by Iroquois reckoning, to pass on critical lineage membership and identity to their children, which male lineage members could not.[7]

In addition to being the primary cultivators, the women of the longhouse were also responsible for the preparation of the main meal, cooked over several fires arranged down the central corridor, including thick corn stew, one of the major staples of their diet. Male residents of the longhouse, unmarried lineage sons and the spouses of lineage daughters, made economic contributions to the longhouse in the form of meat brought home from hunting, fishing, or trading expeditions. Men primarily hunted deer, bear, and passenger pigeon. The matron of the longhouse portioned out both the vegetable and meat resources to the resident component families. The position of matron was based on seniority in the lineage and household, as well as on her talents.

Figure 4.5. Seneca man collecting herbs for medicine, Allegany Reservation, 1940. (William Fenton)

In the United States, much of the scholarly research on marriage and family has focused on the different contributions of husbands and wives in what is commonly recognized as the "traditional" division of labor in American marriages. By the *family wage ideology*—which developed with industrialization in the nineteenth century—husbands took jobs beyond the home in the "workplace," factories and offices, where their work was waged. Wives worked at home, the "domestic domain," where they performed essential although unwaged work associated with child rearing, housekeeping, and managing the domestic economy. The heyday of the family wage division of labor occurred in the 1950s, when three-fifths of American families achieved it.[8]

Many analyses of the American family note that the work done by husbands and wives is considered equally important to the family ideologically. However, the wage value of men's contribution to the family creates a popular perception that the work of spouses is different—both equal and unequal at the same time. In horticultural societies, by contrast, "different and equal" often most accurately characterizes the nature of the subsistence contributions of husband and wife to their family. The Iroquois are a prime ethnographic case wherein husbands and wives, working at very different economic activities, were considered as engaged in work that was both complementary and equal.[9]

KINSHIP, MARRIAGE, AND POLITICS

The pattern of postmarital residence in traditional Iroquois society in which the groom relocates to the bride's mother's longhouse has the effect, across time and generations, of removing sons of the lineage from the longhouse, leaving in *matrilocal* residence the daughters of the lineage, who remain living with the older women of the lineage. This residence practice thus has the effect of placing daughters of the lineage in co-residence in the longhouse. Matrilocal residence together with matrilineal kinship reproduces one of the key features of Iroquois social life, the organization of families, relatives, and households around the female descent line. Each girl born into the lineage remains with her family for a lifetime, never leaving the household and support of her mother and sisters.

Matrilineages, as in the case of Chinese patrilineages, were subsumed within greater kinship groups, called *clans*. In the Iroquois case, two or more matrilineages belonged to one clan, identified by a totem animal that came to symbolize it. Matriclans were known by this totem animal, and a matrlineage belonging to it shared a common identity and historical connection with all other lineages of that clan. In the Chinese case and most other cases with both clans and lineages, distinct lineages are assumed to share a common ancestor or ancestress. This chain of descent, which cannot actually be demonstrated, nonetheless constitutes a powerful common identity. In the Iroquois case, clan membership and identity is more critical in the arrangement of marriage than the lineage, as it was required that people marry outside their clan, not just their lineage.

Among both the Iroquois and the Chinese, kinship was one of the factors both shaping and limiting the field of potential candidates for marriage and in the Iroquois case, for high political office, as well. A bear clan woman could not marry a man of that same clan, even though they might be from different lineages within that clan, with no known blood tie. Such a marriage would be considered incestuous. The requirement that spouses be of different clans is called *clan exogamy* and is one way a kinship system regulates marriage in society.

Clans were based on both kinship and political organization within Iroquois tribes or "nations," as they were known to early generations of Europeans and subsequently, to Americans. Clans were both quasi-kinship units as well as political units within the Iroquois tribes. They were named, and many clan designations were shared across tribes, reflecting perhaps a common origin and history for all the Iroquois tribes. But not all clans occurred within every tribe. Only the bear, turtle, and wolf clans were recognized in all six tribes.

The term *tribe* within anthropological currency has no pejorative connotations but describes a particular kind of political organization, characterizing many rank societies practicing horticulture or pastoralism. Tribal organization describes a polity in which component social or kinship groups of approximate equivalent standing can on occasion and out of necessity align themselves with the other equivalent units. Thus, within Iroquois society, the different component tribes shared a common identity in the greater Iroquois confederacy. It is known that the original five

Iroquois tribes that joined to forge the confederacy—the Onondaga, Seneca, Mohawk, Oneida, and Cayuga—shared a common linguistic base or origin. As it has been historically reconstructed, prior to the arrival of Europeans, these five related tribes, who had been territorial rivals in more recent history, laid aside their differences to unite in a confederacy of tribes, sometimes called *league*. Later, they admitted the Tuscarora tribe, thus creating the six Iroquois tribe confederacy. These tribes, united in common purpose, for territorial defense or aggression, for example, were a potent political force with which to reckon.

The confederacy was the highest level of political organization. Each of the member tribes, with one exception, was represented at the league council by male chiefs, who held inherited titles belonging to lineages, within specific clans within the tribe; the late-joining Tuscarora tribe was allotted none. Furthermore, clans were not equally represented within tribes. And not every matrilineage within a clan held chiefly titles. In short, constituent tribes of the confederacy were represented by a different set number of chiefs, the titles actually being invested within specific clans within that tribe and traditionally held by one of the component matrilineages.

Although the titles to chiefly position were named, ranked, and varied in their significance, all were inherited through the female descent line, inherited within one matrilineage, passing through the line from generation to generation to the sons of the matrilineage. For example, an Onondaga man who inherited a chiefly title within his mother's matrilineage could not pass that title on to his biological son. By the reckoning practice of matrilineal peoples, sons were not born to their father's lineage but to their mother's. Thus, a man's son, although recognized as his, was not his heir and could not inherit from him. A father might give him gifts, but he could not bestow his inherited title to him.

Through Lewis Henry Morgan's writings on the Iroquois, nineteenth-century Americans and Europeans were exposed for the first time to matrilineal kinship. Especially startling to them was the relationship of father and son, as suggested through the Iroquois system of inheritance. It seemed to them to defy nature and the just claim of a son to his father's estate. For some, Morgan's ethnography described a primitive Iroquois "matriarchy," in which wives ruled over husbands.[10] Matrilineal logic was not easy for these nineteenth-century observers, inheriting as they did a more male-focused family and kinship system, the legacy of agrarian societies.

Female lineage elders—especially longhouse matrons—played a pivotal role in determining which of the lineage sons, eligible by age and descent, would inherit the title vacated by the death of a chief. The possible heirs to the title would be the deceased's brothers or male cousins—sons of mother's sisters—who were also members of the deceased's lineage and of an appropriate age to govern. From the pool of possible heirs, the women of the lineage made the actual selection, with considerable influence exerted by the matrons. Typically, one of the favored candidates would in the end receive the endorsement of the assembled women of the lineage and clan. The name of the candidate was then taken by a matron first to the chiefs of that tribe. With their endorsement, she submitted the candidate's name to the gathered chiefs representing half of the tribes of the league and then to the other

Figure 4.6. Seneca family resettled in Oklahoma, early twentieth century. (Frank Speck)

half—all according to a fixed protocol.[11] Finally, all 50 chiefs convened to ratify the selection of new chief. After deliberation and endorsement, the candidate was sworn in to his new duties and station in a special ceremony. Without the endorsement of all chiefs, a nomination was withdrawn and a new meeting called by the women of the lineage and clan to choose a new candidate.

Unlike political decision making within state societies (e.g., traditional Chinese society), with their formal hierarchy of bureaucrats and courts that issued orders and rendered decisions that were ultimately backed by the force of the army and emperor, decision making among the Iroquois more closely compares with the !Kung San case. Even though the Iroquois had formal political leaders, that is, male chiefs, they reached decision by consensus; they collectively had nothing resembling the ultimate power of states to back decisions by armed force. Chiefs in most horticultural societies led by enabling or facilitating consensus, through persuasive arguments leading at last to a collective decision reflecting the minds of the people. Political decisions were made only by reaching agreement among all assembled chiefs at the council, after hours of oratory, discussion, and debate. Iroquois chiefs were known for their eloquent, often lengthy speeches, and oratorical skill was held in much esteem by the people, reminiscent of the much-admired !Kung San mediation skills.

Two levels of council meetings were held: the confederacy council attended by the chiefs of all tribes and the tribal councils attended by the chiefs of individual tribes. The first met to deliberate matters pertaining to the welfare of the entire confederacy, such as making decisions with regard to war or major trade relations.

Figure 4.7. From longhouse to ranch-style house. Family and friends cool off between dances, Allegany Reservation, 1934. (William Fenton)

The tribal councils met separately to discuss business relating only to the tribe. At both levels of council, the chiefs and appointed speakers were recognized and rose to present their case. At neither council were women included as formal delegates or representatives or even scheduled speakers. Nonetheless, a matron of a matrilineage might stand and wait to be recognized; she would be heard, for chiefs and the people respected female elders for their knowledge and experience in life and lineage affairs. Indeed, in the Iroquois matron was vested the power to initiate impeachment proceedings against a chief not living up to the responsibilities of his title.

In this and all matrilineal societies, male political authority was determined by birth into specific female descent lines. Thus, a chief's authority was not based in a separate male world but was conditioned by the place of women within the descent line that underwrote his power. Women of the line exercised considerable influence within their extended family household and lineage. A male chief's authority could best be described as contingent, based on his ability to persuade, influence, and cajole other chiefs—and the people themselves—to back his position on a particular issue. On marriage, even a chief left his house, which was his mother's longhouse, to go and live with "strangers," including not only his wife but all the women of her lineage resident in her longhouse.

RESIDENCE AND THE MEANING OF MARRIAGE

The Iroquois marriage ceremony, as Morgan's account indicates, was modest and did not dramatize any dislocation or alienation from a groom's natal lineage and longhouse. This simple ceremony would be characteristic of all weddings, including a chief's. Marriage was arranged by the mothers of bride and groom, women belonging to different clans and perhaps to different tribes within the confederacy, too; they may have met at council gatherings or on important ritual occasions attended by many clans of many tribes, such as the Green Corn or Harvest Festivals. As friends or acquaintances, and with relatives living in different clans, each would gather enough information about the personal qualities of the young person under consideration to make her decision on the wisdom of the match. Especially important in horticultural societies was a reputation for hard work. The labor required to make a living by horticulture far exceeded that demanded by foraging.

When both mothers were satisfied, they gave their assent to the marriage of their son and daughter without consulting either. As in both !Kung San and Chinese marriages, affection between the engaged couple was not considered a positive recommendation for marriage. Nor was it believed advantageous in the adaptation to married life that both the bride and groom must make within the context of a longhouse, based on cooperative living and labor under the matron's watchful eye. Traditionally, mothers sought to arrange a marriage between a bride slightly older than the groom, both of whom were young adults. The slight age disparity in favor of the Iroquois bride was believed to provide a groom with a companion who was already experienced in the affairs of life.

When without fanfare the groom arrived at the bride's mother's longhouse, the bride served him the customary welcoming bowl of hominy that marked his entry into both marriage and residence in her house. In this ethnographic case, the groom was in some respects in a similar position to the Chinese bride in that he left his family and home. He, not his wife, was the "outsider" among his wife's family's relatives, including not only the women of the matrilineage and their spouses but the unmarried or divorced sons of the lineage. As the newcomer, the groom was in a similar position to the Chinese bride. He was watched by all of the longhouse residents, who were concerned that he meet the obligations of a husband in his new marriage and home. He was expected to regularly provide the house matron with the products of his hunting and fishing expeditions, respect the residents of the house, and provide his wife and her line with children.[12]

Sons of the lineage who were residing with their wives and children in other lineage longhouses, perhaps in other villages, also took the measure of the new husband. This was not an impossible feat because in matrilineal societies, villages were usually closely spaced to one another in order to accommodate what can be described as the dual obligations of males as both brothers and husbands. This situation creates a critical difference between Chinese and Iroquois ethnographic cases with regard to marriage and the position of the in-marrying spouse. Iroquois husbands, in contrast to Chinese wives, were not completely absorbed into the homes and lines of their spouse, and thus not alienated from their natal family or lineage. Among the Iroquois, both daughters and sons remained important members and participants in their natal families. Daughters were the means to biologically continue the female descent line, the backbone of the family and lineage, whereas sons continued as guardians or overseers of the affairs of both.

Despite their shift in residence with marriage, men remained full members of their natal longhouses and lineages, suffering no loss in status or station with relocation. Although a husband might in time develop a companionate marriage with his wife and affection for his children, his primary orientation remained his home lineage. His membership there was not weakened by marriage and matrilocal residence. Indeed, his first obligation was to see to the security and welfare of his sisters and their children, who would continue the lineage. In short, an Iroquois husband—like all husbands in matrilineal societies—was essential to the continuation of *his* lineage, which was the lineage of his sister and mother in another village.

In the case of the Chinese bride, who moved into her husband's father's home in a different clan and village, she served no further purpose to her natal family. She could not provide it with the sons it needed to continue the male descent line, and she could not die in her natal home. Marriage gave a Chinese wife a new male descent line (her husband's) that she could serve, fate willing, by producing sons to continue it. Divorce was rare, except in the poorer classes where ideals did not matter as much. In the event she was ordered to leave her husband's home, she had no place to which to return. Wives relocated in patrilocal residence in many societies suffered loss of place in the families they left, which weakened their position both in their marriage and in their marital home.

Iroquois grooms in matrilocal residence, on the other hand, had not only a welcoming home to which to return but were never "transferred" in any real sense. Their primary identification and obligation remained always the same: the home and lineage of their mother. Thus, a husband in Iroquois society was in a very different position than the Chinese bride; he could return at any time for extended visits or if his marriage should fail. In the event of divorce, he would pick up his few belongings and return to his lineage's longhouse, where he would remain until he left to marry again.

If an Iroquois husband and wife divorced, he was the one to leave. Divorce meant that he not only left a troubled marriage but his own children, too. As members of their mother's house and lineage, they remained with her—he might be unhappy at parting from his children, but child custody and their place in society were never at issue. If the father was of the beaver clan and mother of the turtle, the children were unquestionably all turtle.

In each society, children are taught who they are, where they belong, and what family is. In Iroquois society, fathers, according to the historical sources, were affectionate to their own children and played an important role in their upbringing and in teaching their sons essential skills, particularly the skills needed to hunt well. In the event of divorce, a man returned to a longhouse and to his sisters' children, for whom he was always an important role model. Because the Iroquois lived in communal residential arrangements, children were never deprived of the concerned and

Figure 4.8. Seneca man pounding corn meal, Allegany Reservation, New York, 1933. (William Fenton)

Figure 4.9. Seneca woman at Coldspring, New York, begins a twined cornhusk basket, 1933. She was the last of the Seneca basket twiners. (William Fenton)

Figure 4.10. Seneca woman at Coldspring, New York, leaches hominy corn with wood ashes to make corn soup, 1933. (William Fenton)

Figure 4.11. Making herbal medicine, 1930s. (William Fenton)

affectionate attention of an adult male, including their mother's brothers. Maternal uncles played an important role in the lives of their nephews, who were technically *their* heirs and successors in the lineage; a man's nephews were potential candidates for any chiefly title he might hold.

Nonetheless, divorce was not treated lightly. The mothers of the couple assumed the responsibility for mediating any marital crisis that might arise. After all, marriage was not just a union of a husband and wife but of two clans as well. The mothers' duty and interest were to attempt to reconcile the couple for the sake of personal, family, and clan interests. Still, a notable feature of Iroquois and other matrilineal societies is that, once reconciliation attempts had failed and a marriage was over, there were no great obstacles or public outcry against divorce and no stigma attached to either the divorced husband or wife. Neither suffered diminished lifestyle or reputation; neither was disadvantaged economically because both a divorced wife and husband always had a primary identification and membership in their natal lineage. Upon divorce, the husband moved out and returned to his mother's longhouse, and life resumed.

Anthropologists who have worked in other matrilineal societies—including the Trobriand Islanders of New Guinea—have remarked on the relative absence of domestic dispute beyond a certain pitch in matrilineal societies because neither husband nor wife on marriage is alienated from their family by great property exchanges or ideology that deems one party expendable.[13] In a matrilineal society, sons are seen as having a permanent place and role in their mother's lineage and a critical role in the lives of their sisters' children. Men in matrilineal societies thus have a lifelong dual familial responsibility: to the children of his wife and most important, of his sister.

BROTHERS AND SISTERS, HUSBANDS AND WIVES

Among the Iroquois, and in matrilineal societies in general, the relationship between siblings was extremely close. Among sisters, a cooperative relationship was critical and nurtured from youngest childhood. Growing up in a longhouse, sisters were raised knowing they would always live together, working and supporting each other in the best interests of the family and lineage. They would continue to reside in the longhouse after marriage and would be present to care for aging family members. Loyalty, cooperation, and consensus were important family values promoted within the longhouse. Older women residents—mother, aunts, grandmother—wielded influence and authority in the home and set an example as strong role models.

The relationship between brothers and sisters was also extremely close, and even after marriage, brothers continued to participate actively in the lives of their sisters and their sisters' children and in the affairs of the lineage. In some matrilineal societies, such as among the Trobrianders, a brother materially supports his sister, her husband, and their children—his heirs—by cultivating a yam garden for her, in which he produces a major portion of their annual yam holdings. (Yams among the Trobrianders are a staple of the diet, item of exchange, and symbol of success.) The primacy and centrality of the brother-sister relationship among the Iroquois and Trobrianders seems to rival the social and emotional emphasis that Americans reserve for the bond between couples in marriage.

In the study of matrilineal societies, anthropologists have discovered that to focus primarily on the bond between husband and wife in marriage actually distorts the important family dynamics that link the lives and futures of brothers and sisters, as well as mothers and daughters.[14] In these societies, important relationships cross the boundaries of nuclear families, creating larger, meaningful family contexts.

Marriage in matrilineal societies shapes a conjugal relationship that has been described as being of a relatively easy nature.[15] Marriage was not arranged to sustain an emotional attachment but in large part took its meaning from the greater family and kinship systems in which it was embedded. Similar to the Chinese case, marriage was arranged to create a relationship between two different lineages and clans, creating affinal ties that can be used as social, economic, and political resources. Spouses in these cultural contexts cannot be viewed as individuals or free agents but are persons whose identity is to a great extent taken from the larger kinship groups in which they are born; marriage serves to promote those larger kinship interests.

Thus, in a matrilineal society such as the Iroquois, the general tenor of the relationship between husbands and wives can be characterized as cooperative and companionate. It does not bear the same kind of emotional investment (or burden) characteristic of marriage, for instance, in American society. It also contrasts with the situation in many patrilineal-patrilocal societies wherein kinship, marriage, and residence systems together shape a conjugal relationship in which one spouse (the wife) is denied any continuing role in her own family and lineage.

The power of residence in shaping the experience of spouses in Iroquois marriage is dramatically highlighted in the contrast with the patrilineal-patrilocal Chinese. In traditional Chinese society, residence strengthened the position of husbands in marriage and society but undercut the position of wives, isolating them in the husband's home and village. Residence practice was no less powerful in creating the more equitable experience of spouses in marriage in Iroquois society. Everywhere, then, residence practice is a major cultural force in the making of marriage.

■ ■ ■

In the case of the Nyinba of Nepal (ethnic Tibetans discussed in chapter 5), their practice of patrilineal kinship and patrilocal residence appears at first to create a family and household reminiscent of China. As in China, the economy is agrarian, supporting a hierarchy of social and economic classes, as well as genders. Unlike China, however, marriage with patrilocal residence does not introduce a Nyinba bride into an established domestic hierarchy of wives but rather a hierarchy of husbands, leading to a number of questions: How does the practice of such polyandry shape the meaning of marriage for a Nyinba wife and her several husbands (who are brothers)? What is the relationship between marriage and high alpine agriculture in Nyinba society? How is Nyinba ethnic identity and the hierarchy of social classes reproduced by polyandry?

5

Marriage among Tibetans:
The Nyinba of Nepal

In 1983, the largest Nyinba household numbered eighteen men and women, of three generations. The most senior generation included three polyandrously married brothers, who ranged in age from fifty-two to sixty, and their common wife, who was fifty-nine at the time. Living with them were five of their sons, aged twenty to forty, and their sons' wife, who then was thirty-five. The other household members included one unmarried teenaged daughter, three grandsons, and four granddaughters. These men had another son who had partitioned [divorced] fifteen years earlier and three daughters who were married and living with their husbands.

Nancy Levine
Nepal, 1988[1]

Tibetan society has had a grip on the Western imagination, as well as the attention of anthropologists, since its marriage practice came to the attention of outsiders. In the Tibetan practice of fraternal polyandry, brothers collectively marry one wife. Among the world's documented diverse customary marriage systems, the practice of fraternal polyandry is one of the most rarely occurring and is found exclusively in South Asia, primarily in Tibet, Nepal, and India. The Tibetan practice, both in Tibet and in ethnic Tibetan communities in Nepal, has been the subject of much ethnographic research and provides the focus of this exploration of the practice and meaning of fraternal polyandry.[2]

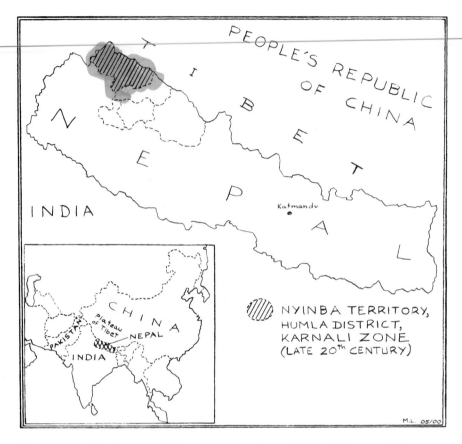

Map 5.1. Map showing area of Tibetan Nyinba settlement in Nepal, late twentieth century.

For Westerners, the practice of polyandry seems to demand an explanation in a way that polygyny does not. For a woman to marry several husbands who are brothers seems almost unnatural because from the Western cultural perspective and marriage practice, marriage means love and sex are shared exclusively with one's spouse, and especially so for a wife.

Like marriage with matrilocal residence among the matrilineal Iroquois, fraternal polyandry seems from a Western perspective to advantage the wife and disadvantage the husband in marriage. Polyandry was especially subject to wild speculative theories in the nineteenth century. Social evolutionists sought to assign this "obviously" premodern form of marriage to a more primitive stage in the cultural progress of humankind. Fraternal polyandry could not, by this reckoning, be in any sense modern because it was not descriptive of marriage in Western societies.

Some of these evolutionary theories can shed light on Western prejudice. One example of this prejudice is reflected in the nineteenth-century popular interpretation that polyandry must be a "survival" from a primitive cultural past, when group marriage was customary and descent could only be traced through women. How could a biological father be determined? How could he assume patriarchal control of his sons and inheritance when paternity was unknown? These were the kinds of questions that framed the West's initial encounter with the practice of polyandry.[3]

Tibetan polyandry as a marriage system has been best ethnographed among the Nyinba of Nepal. The Nyinba are ethnic Tibetans who settled in northwestern Nepal in the seventeenth century. Polyandry from the perspective of family structure and process has not been as intensively studied in Tibet proper as among the Tibetans resident in Nepal, in part because access to Tibet has been restricted for both anthropologists and other Westerners since the occupation of Tibet by the People's Republic of China in 1959.

POLYANDRY IN AGRARIAN SOCIETY

Nyinba traditionally practiced plow agriculture in one of the most striking and physically challenging environments in the world, in the high valleys of the Himalayan Mountains of the Tibetan plateau. Typical Nyinba villages are established at elevations often more than 9,000 feet, with agricultural fields stretching as high as 11,000 feet, among the world's most elevated farmland. This rugged, mountainous environment is an especially difficult one in which to carve out fields for intensive cultivation and a challenge to any agrarian tradition.

This rare environment in which the Nyinba practice both alpine agriculture and polyandry has provided the primary focus for anthropologists' study of marriage in that society. Because arable land is at a premium and all of it long improved and claimed, the demographic effects of polyandry in this environment have been analyzed as a functional means of curtailing the growth of population.

Consider a typical Nyinba marriage in which three brothers marry one wife. The advantage of this marital scheme, whereby several husbands—the full set of brothers in a family—marry one wife, is readily apparent for this environment. Monogamy would be a much more "costly" marital regime, producing many more children, all dependent on a fixed land base. Thus one of the demographic outcomes of polyandry is the reduction in the number of children born, creating families and households with relatively stable composition over the generations. Migration into Nyinba communities is negligible.

Traditionally, stable family size has been the point of entry for anthropological analyses of Tibetan fraternal polyandry. The demographic repercussions of polyandry are cast by some anthropologists as the continuing motivation for its practice among the Nyinba and other alpine agriculturists. That polyandry may have originally developed within this specific environment as an adaptive response to extreme environmental constraints on agriculture and subsistence in general seems probable. Whether one can assume, based on the probable causes for the rise of polyandry, that those first causes drive its continuing practice remains an open question. Does the fact that it maintains a stable household population, preventing rising demand on fixed

Figure 5.1. A village sits adjacent to the terraced fields owned by the men of the Nyinba household. Men are responsible for plowing the fields and planting them with buckwheat, amaranth, and wheat. (Thomas L. Kelly)

agricultural resources, mean that contemporary polyandry is based on an ongoing awareness of economic benefits? Do Nyinba families in each household and generation ask themselves whether this time they can afford to marry their sons with monogamy? In short, is polyandry a continuing economic calculation?

OF HOUSES AND LINES

As in the Chinese case, an important part of the cultural context for understanding Nyinba marriage practice and meaning is the agrarian economy, based on plow agriculture. The Nyinba, like the Chinese, practice both patrilineal kinship and patrilocal residence. Land, although scarce, is the basis of agriculture and also the foundation for social hierarchy. At the center of the organization and management of agricultural land among the Nyinba is the household, or *trongba*. As in the Chinese case, the family and household is the fundamental unit of production and consumption, and members share in a common domestic economy. It is also the lowest level of political organization.

Among the Nyinba, the household is based on patrilineal kinship, and family sons are its focus across the generations. Patrilocal residence here has the effect of dispersing family daughters at marriage into their husband's home. Sons, by

Figure 5.2. A Nyinba household composed of several brothers can diversify economically. One or more brothers embark on seasonal trading expeditions to Tibet, supplementing their household economy, based on farming, thereby bringing greater prosperity to all. (Thomas L. Kelly)

contrast, remain in the family and household. All family members, whether they are currently resident in the household or temporarily away on family business, contribute to the household economy and are supported by it, again similar to the Chinese case.

One important contrast to the Chinese case is that the Nyinba household continues beyond the life of any one generation of sons. The family estate—house and land—is not regularly divided among sons on the death of the senior generation. In traditional Chinese society, although the division of the family estate was not the cultural ideal, certain factors pushed co-resident brothers toward family division, the most important being the practice of marriage itself.

In the Chinese case, the centrifugal forces of the extended family dynamics created by the marriages of the sons—and multiple marriages by sons of the elite in that polygynous society—meant that division and separation was the usual outcome upon the death of the family patriarch. Wives, as strangers in their husband's home, were each motivated to protect and promote the interest of their own uterine family from the rival uterine families competing for resources in a common domestic economy. Wives married to the different brothers therefore saw division of the family estate as the solution to this problem, and each encouraged her husband to take his share at the death of the father.

Each brother in Chinese society inherited equally from his father, a custom called per stirpes inheritance. The overall effect of this system in the context of the divisive currents of the Chinese family was the division of the estate into smaller shares, thus causing fragmentation of the land holdings in each generation. Sons in succeeding generations, therefore, had a more difficult time re-creating the lifestyle of their parents if they could not substantially add to the inherited land through hard work and good luck. Thus downward social mobility was characteristic of the experience of many Chinese families over a few generations.

Although the same inheritance system is in place in the Nyinba case, it has stronger normative pressures against family division. In addition, family dynamics do not as regularly create pressures for family division, setting one brother against another. Instead, tremendous cultural energy is focused on avoiding the division of the household and estate because fragmentation in this environment could only mean certain economic disaster.

Pressures against division are so strong that the household is described as "corporate," with a life of its own, continuing beyond any one generation of sons. In this manner, the entire estate is preserved as an intact resource base for the next generation of household members. Thus, family and household within Nyinba society work to maintain a consistent land base in an environment in which new land to clear is virtually unavailable. The greater longevity of an undivided household among the Nyinba is one of the achievements of their very different marriage practice.

The Nyinba family, like its Chinese counterpart, is based on the economic contribution of sons behind plows. Both family and household organizations in each society focus on a male descent and the localizing of sons in permanent residence with their parents. Sons in both societies were the heirs and future of the family. In the Tibetan case, however, male descent lines are not as dominant as in the Chinese case. The latter, supported by the practice of male ancestor worship, gave the line a life beyond any one generation of sons. In short, in the Chinese example, the male descent line took precedence over the family estate.

In the Tibetan case, although the primacy of male descent shaped family and society, the descent line is subsumed within the household. The next generation of sons would inherit the estate as a set of brothers, who would in turn collectively provide sons to continue line and family into the future. In contrast to the Chinese, the Nyinba household has a more dominant cultural presence than the male descent line. All of this was made possible because a cohort of brothers in a household married one wife.

THE ORGANIZATION OF WORK IN MARRIAGE

Nyinba brothers are raised to cooperate both in marriage and in the labor to sustain the household. Two, three, or more brothers might depend on the same land base, but Tibetans built economic success out of diversifying the economic activities of brothers. In the general division of male labor in the household, at least one brother is needed in agricultural work; the family fields have to be plowed in preparation for planting buckwheat, the primary staple, as well as other grains, including barley, millet, amaranth, and wheat, and the terrace walls supporting the fields require regular maintenance. Another son specializes in small-scale cattle herding to meet household demands for meat, butter, and compost for the fields, as well as for animals to use in trade. Yaks, and perhaps a few sheep, are also kept by the household. To live the best life, however, a household needs a brother engaged in the highly lucrative, long-distance salt trade, traveling with pack animals between Tibet and India, trading salt for grain.

Thus people's everyday experience in the family and community taught them that households with many men (brothers and sons) were in a position to succeed and lead lives of prosperity. A household with no son, or only one surviving to adulthood, would be severely economically disadvantaged. A *trongba* needed multiple sons to pursue the strategy of diversification into the different occupational niches to achieve the good life.

The sharing of one wife is another striking instance of brothers' cooperation and loyalty among themselves. In the Nyinba practice of polyandry, one wife marries a set of brothers and moves into their household with patrilocal residence. Although a Western outsider might expect that the lone wife enjoys an elevated status within the household with so many spouses to attend to her needs, the ethnographic reality is far different.

The division of labor between the sexes in the family and the general cultural devaluation of what is seen as "women's work" reflect the dominant preference for males in this patrilineal society. Although some agricultural tasks are shared by both husbands and wife at the time grain is harvested, there is otherwise a fairly rigid division of labor in which work assigned to a wife is considered to be less

prestigious. In fact, a wife assumes the majority of the work associated with cultivation after plowing, including the critical but onerous task of weeding the fields.
She also performs all of the work of grain processing—winnowing, husking, roast-
ing, and storing. In addition to these, a wife is assigned all the domestic work surrounding cooking and meal preparation, hauling water for the household, child
care, and the laundry of multiple husbands. In prosperous traditional households,
this last list of chores was undertaken by slaves, who were manumitted in Nepal
in 1926. The work of slaves was considered by nature demeaned, further under-
scoring the lesser cultural evaluation of a wife's own economic contribution within
the Nyinba household.

THE DYNAMICS OF POLYANDRY

The selection of a wife for the brothers of the household is the prerogative of the
eldest brother. Through a process of courting a number of girls in the village, he
selects one who is attractive to him and with whom he may develop a sexual relationship, but who must also meet several criteria to marry into the household as
wife. First, she must be a member of another line of descent and clan. Among the
Nyinba, male descent lines are the focus of households and the group of households
occupying a village hamlet. These localized groups of households sharing a common line of descent are considered to be one branch of a clan. While Nyinba male
descent lines each belong to named clans, the direct relationship between the different branches of a clan cannot be traced. It doesn't need to be; it is assumed. As
in most societies with clan organizations, the Nyinba recognize a common found-
ing ancestor, but no clan branch can show direct descent from him.

In addition, reminiscent of the Chinese case, the households united in marriage
must be of relatively equivalent economic and social standing. Traditionally, households were ranked in a hierarchy, from commoner households to the aristocratic.[4]
The elders of both households must also agree to the marriage, which requires the
services of relatives to manage the sensitive negotiations. Horoscopes are consulted
and matched; for marriage negotiations to proceed, a bride's horoscope has to match
at least one of her husbands'. In addition, the grooms' family makes a gift of cash,
which is paid to the bride's family and used to assemble a small dowry, including
household goods such as pots, pans, and tools, as well as perhaps livestock. (Traditionally, more elaborate dowries might include slaves, given by the wealthiest families, to accompany the bride to her new home.) The cost of the bridewealth is sur-
passed by the cost of the wedding celebration itself, stretching several days of feasting,
drinking, singing, and dancing by the assembled guests. As part of the marriage ritual, representatives of the grooms' family stage a mock capture of the bride, who is
"kidnapped" from her parents' home. As she prepares to leave her family as a ritual
"captive" bride, a daughter will receive a blessing from her father, who daubs her
forehead with butter. The grooms' party escorting her will later stop on the trail to
allow her a last glance back at her old home, before continuing the trek to her new

Figure 5.3. Nyinba houses are typically built of stone masonry in three levels. The primary family living area is on the second level, which contains the kitchen, sleeping rooms, and some storage areas. The bottom level is occupied by animals owned by the household. The upper story houses a ceremonial shrine and provides safekeeping for family valuables. The levels are linked by ladders. The flat rooftops provide storage space for crops, as well as threshing grounds for grains and play space for children. (Thomas L. Kelly)

village, home, and husbands who await her. For the parents of the grooms, who have saved for years for the occasion, the wedding celebration represents an investment in the marriages of several sons (perhaps as many as five) and the future of an undivided household.[5] Frequently, poorer families encourage their eldest son to elope.

Married and living with two or more husbands in a household based on loyalty and cooperation among brothers requires management. Eventually, the common wife is responsible for being sexually available to all of her husbands. The usual dynamic characterizing conjugal relations within a polyandrous marriage is that the eldest brother enjoys an early and fairly exclusive honeymoon period. Given the age disparity among a set of brothers, it is not uncommon for the youngest brother(s) to be too young to assume sexual relations. But each brother who is mature is welcomed into the marriage, as are the younger brothers as they come of age.[6]

All brothers are expected to be full partners in the marriage, and it is the wife's responsibility to see that each brother shares time with her in a rotational fashion. She must be careful to include each brother equally, sharing her affections and seeking to minimize signs of any favoritism on her part. She will be the first one approached to improve her relations with any of her husbands who feels slighted in her attentions.

Cultural protocols have developed to diminish the risk of conflict arising out of delicate domestic situations. Sexual access to the wife by any of her husbands is

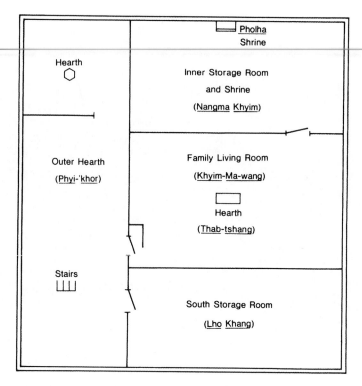

Figure 5.4. Traditional design of Nyinba household living quarters, second floor. The wife's bedroom is located upstairs.

not a matter left strictly to chance. Although one or more husbands may be temporarily absent from home, for those remaining, "whose turn" may be established by the wife herself. Perhaps over the morning meal, a wife will indicate which of her husbands will sleep with her that evening, trying to achieve the fairest rotation of husbands possible. Alternatively, because a wife has a room of her own in which she always sleeps, a husband's shoes left outside her door will signal his brother that he is too late. Or the key to her room, typically kept on a ledge by her door, may be missing, a clear sign that one husband has already claimed their wife for the evening.[7] However, a wife and her husbands work together to create a satisfactory marriage for all; everyone, including parents, wishes to avert conflict among husbands that would lead to the division or "partitioning" of the household.

SONS AND FATHERS

In the family, the focus is on sons and raising them to be loyal to each other for the sake of the undivided polyandrous household; this is a part of what it means to be

Figure 5.5. A Nyinba wife, front left, threshes buckwheat beside her mother-in-law, right foreground. One of her five husbands is seated in the back with a raised mallet. (Thomas L. Kelly)

Nyinba. Sons are raised to place cooperation among brothers above competition. In a sense, they learn to sublimate feelings of jealousy for the sake of the family. The cultural values that the Nyinba and other Tibetans esteem are produced and reproduced across the generations by preparing sons for a collective, cooperative marriage.

The focus on sons and their place in marriage, the line, and the household comes at the expense of daughters. There is a marked difference in family response to the birth of sons and daughters, the former bringing joy and the latter disappointment. With the future of the family and the household dependent on adult sons, boys receive the most attention and the best food, while daughters can, in comparison, suffer relative neglect, for example, receiving less nursing as infants. Son preference has an effect on the rate at which girls survive to adulthood, which is lower than for boys.

The assignment of paternity among children to specific fathers is in Tibet in general not as significant an issue as it is among the Nyinba. This situation can be explained as a result of the different inheritance customs in traditional Tibetan society and in contemporary Nepal.[8] By traditional Tibetan practice, a per capita inheritance rule governs the division of estate property, should such a rupture be unavoidable. All children inherit equally—meaning sons of the household—but daughters

Figure 5.6. Women spend their winter days weaving handspun wool from their sheep. (Thomas L. Kelly)

are entitled to a lesser share as dowry. With the per stirpes inheritance regime imposed by law in Nepal, sons inherit equally, but only from their recognized father, creating the situation whereby a man without a recognized son might find himself without complete support in his later years. Or he might see his theoretical share of his own father's inheritance absorbed by the sons of his brother because he himself lacks a known heir. The traditional meaning of *father* among Tibetans can be seen to shift in the context of a different inheritance system in Nepal. A brother in a polyandrous marriage in Nepal needs to identify a particular son as his to gain greater security in the household. In a sense, the different inheritance law in place in Nepal creates a new basis for tension and rivalry among brothers in a polyandrous marriage. Thus, contemporary Nyinba polyandrous marriage needs to produce sons with recognized fathers. (Interestingly, fathers and their recognized sons do not call each other by any special term of reference; children refer to all their mother's husbands as "father.")

The responsibility for such recognition rests with the common wife. The Nyinba believe that a wife knows when she has conceived and which of her husbands fathered the child. Wives keep track of their monthly cycles, and in some cases one brother might be weeks away on a salt-trading expedition. Still, the assignment of paternity is politics at the most intimate level of the family. While, from one perspective, a wife can be seen to wield domestic power in naming the father of her child from among his brothers, she also bears the responsibility for her decision. Nyinba admit that a wife sometimes apportions paternity to achieve greater satisfaction among all of her husbands in her marriage or to repair a strained relationship with one particular husband.

The Nyinba believe that the best future for an adult daughter is marriage, but polyandry creates a situation in which many fewer daughters are able to marry, resulting in a surplus of adult unmarried women (daughters). An adult daughter is by custom entitled to a dowry or maintenance in her family, but in reality most families believe a spinster daughter at home will only interfere with her sister-in-law, the wife of her brothers, and the smooth running of the household. Parents, therefore, are not reluctant to marry an older daughter out of Nyinba society to a Nepali husband. In this case, the daughter is virtually assured of little continuing contact with her natal family. Still another parental strategy is to send an unmarried daughter into a life of domestic service.

EXCEPTIONS TO POLYANDRY

Polyandry for the Nyinba serves as a cultural sign of identity, separating them from their monogamous neighbors in greater Nepal. The identification of polyandry with ethnicity in part conditions the Nyinba response to other forms of marriage. Among the Nyinba, all brothers marry with polyandry, regardless of the economic conditions of their household. It is the cultural ideal form of marriage, it is the norm, and it is integral to Nyinba identity. However, some marriages are inherently monogamous. If parents have only one son—whether he is an only son or the sole surviving son—he will by default marry monogamously. The Nyinba consider such a situation to be unfortunate. First, it is just not quite Nyinba to marry without polyandry. Furthermore, people believe that a household dependent on a monogamous marriage cannot prosper, a belief borne out by observation. Without at least two sons, the household cannot pursue the diversified livelihood that will ensure prosperity in the household.

A polyandrous marriage that breaks down can also produce monogamy and trigger what the Nyinba believe to be an inevitable slide into household poverty. Marital rift most often occurs when one husband becomes dissatisfied with the marriage because he does not have as much time with the wife as his brothers or because he and the wife do not have a good relationship. Although most marriages do not fail due to strong normative pressures to support them, statistically, marriages of three or more husbands are more likely to produce one husband who feels slighted by the wife. Everyone in the household will seek to reconcile the wife and her unhappy husband, but the wife assumes much of the responsibility for the marriage's success or failure.

In some cases, the disaffected husband finds a girlfriend in the village and insists to his fathers and brothers to be allowed to marry her into the household as an additional wife. The result would be polygyny—a marriage of a man to plural wives—yielding a complex marriage and a threat to domestic harmony, which everyone seeks to avoid. A second wife is welcomed into a Nyinba marriage, however, if the

Figure 5.7. A Nyinba wedding. The bride's representatives sit singing on the rooftop. Soon they will call the eldest groom forward to daub butter on his head, thus sanctifying the marriage. (Thomas L. Kelly)

Figure 5.8. During the wedding, the grooms' representatives dance in the courtyard of the bride's home, encircled by the bride's representatives, who carry pussy willow staffs as mock protective weapons. (Thomas L. Kelly)

first wife proves unable to have children. In that special case, the brothers will seek out a second wife who ideally is the sister or female cousin of the first. Nyinba believe that cowives are a prelude to divisions among brothers and the household but that wives who share the same blood will be less prone to rivalry and fights. The marriage in the event of infertility is called sororal polygynous polyandry. It is the exception to the general reluctance to permit a second marriage. The Nyinba belief that close kinship creates compatibility stems from their conviction that brothers share "bone" and "blood," which provides a natural basis for cooperation and loyalty. Equally, cowives related by close kinship ties have what is felt to be a natural basis for compatibility.

In the event that one husband wants to introduce a second wife into the marriage because he is unhappy, his candidate will have been selected on the basis of affection and not kinship. Knowing that this marriage will cause trouble for the household, his family will try to dissuade him. The first wife is again urged to improve her relations with this husband, but failing that, the disaffected husband may ultimately force his brothers to agree to the additional marriage. Although the second wife is technically considered a wife for them all, that marriage inevitably proves to be focused on just the one husband. This exclusivity creates a volatile situation for the brothers, as well as for the cowives, who become rivals and find it difficult to cooperate in the domestic chores. No one expects two wives who share no kinship relationship to be able to peacefully share husbands and household.

Figure 5.9. A Nyinba wedding photo. The ten-year-old bride poses with three of her five new husbands, including the youngest husband, who is only seven years old. Her two other husbands were away on a trading expedition at the time of the wedding. (Thomas L. Kelly)

The typical outcome to this unfortunate arrangement is mounting pressure from the exclusive couple to separate from the main household. Nyinba experience this division of the brothers as a failure to live up to Nyinba ideals in marriage. The exclusive couple receives a small house and attached plot to cultivate on a corner of the household property. They are now a monogamously married couple, with a separate domestic economy, although no one expects them to live well because they will be dependent on the labor of only one male. The household will be short of the male labor needed to guarantee it a secure, let alone prosperous, livelihood. Typically, the couple will live out its days in hard work, perhaps leaving sons who might be reabsorbed into the main household at some later date.

In many societies, the collective memory of clans, lineages, and households will erase any exceptions to high tradition. Such is the case for divorce in Nyinba society, which represents a failure to achieve the cultural ideal of household harmony and cooperation. In the event of divorce, a wife's children belong to her husband's line and household. She will remain near them, occupying a small house established on a corner of the property for her residence, or perhaps just an unused room in the barn. In either place, in what is called an "adjunct" residence, she will receive basic maintenance support but will live in relative poverty.

Although a divorced wife can rightfully claim her dowry and return to her natal home, this is primarily an option for a wife without children. The homecoming will not be a welcome one in her natal family, and a divorced wife hopes to leave soon

96

Figure 5.10. In this wedding photo, the bride stands at back on the right. Her five grooms pose in traditional Nyinba wedding finery, wrapped in cloaks of white homespun wool. The five new husbands are brothers—the sons by the two husbands of their mother. (Thomas L. Kelly)

for the home of a new husband. With children, however, a divorced wife will remain near the household of her former husbands to be in close proximity to her children. In time, these lapses in tradition will be forgotten within the formal history of the greater household.

MARRIAGE, HIERARCHY, AND IDENTITY

Reinforcing the interpretation that polyandry is a sign of Nyinba identity—and that monogamy is not—is the practice of marriage among slaves.[9] Before manumission in the early twentieth century, slaves constituted about 1 percent of the population within the Nyinba community. Slaves were considered the chattel property of households and were acquired through purchase, received as dowry in the marriages of wealthy Nyinba, or inherited through patrilineal descent within the household. Slaves were by definition not Nyinba, although many were persons who were ethnically Tibetan and who, due to poverty, had sold themselves (or their fathers or grandfathers had sold themselves) into slavery in Nepal. Through several social processes—including kinship, marriage, and residence—they were transformed into different and "alien" people.

The Nyinba transformed the slaves from people with specific clan, line, and household affiliations and with ties to land and history into people with none of these by removing them from those contexts and turning them into cultural "others." Nyinba considered their slaves to be without clan ancestors and legitimate historical connection to households—they were, after all, "strangers"—thereby depriving them of any relationship to themselves. Over time, slaves and their children were re-created as less than Nyinba, through the work they were assigned in the household of their masters and through their distinctive marriage and kinship practices.

Male and female slaves made important economic contributions to Nyinba households, both performing work that was designated as "women's work." In the wealthy households that could afford them, they hauled water, fetched wood, cared for children, and assisted in cooking and serving meals to family members, all tasks considered exclusively in the domain of a Nyinba wife. Nyinba, and Tibetan households in general, typically suffered from a shortage of women to perform their specific tasks because polyandry restricted the number of adult women in any household. Thus, slaves, although of a demeaned status, were a welcome, albeit expensive, addition to a traditional Tibetan household.

Further separating slaves from any close approximation to ethnic Tibetans, including Nyinba, was the arrangement of their marriage. Owners of slaves sent a male slave off to an appointed wife in an arranged uxorilocal marriage, by which the groom joined the bride in her house. This dwelling was an adjunct household, small quarters befitting of a slave union, and in proximity to the owners' household. Slaves were not permitted to marry by any other residence practice and were particularly forbidden to form a family or household around patrilocal residence. They were also forbidden to marry by polyandry, which was reserved for Nyinba as a mark of their exclusive ethnic identity.

Thus, slave families were typically small, with shallow genealogies and no clan identity to establish them as citizens on a par with members of Nyinba households. With work assigned to them and no concentration of men created by patrilocal residence that might have enabled some economic diversification, they of course remained poor. In effect, enslaved persons were deprived of all the cultural markers—including clans, genealogies, and historical links with land—that would suggest any relationship to Tibetans themselves and any claim to Nyinba identity and privileges. And of course, marriage between Nyinba and slaves was forbidden.

The kinds of social processes found in Nyinba society were characteristic of many agrarian societies, including traditional Chinese society.[10] Particularly highlighted in the Nyinba ethnography is the contribution of the practice of postmarital residence to the cultural construction of ethnic identity. In addition, residence can be clearly seen to both empower and support one spouse, while isolating the other, thus compromising the ability of husbands and wives to achieve an equitable relationship in marriage.

Ultimately, when they were freed in Nepal in 1926, slaves became freedmen who have sought to reverse the previous social processes in an attempt to make themselves more like ethnic Tibetans. Freedmen strategically use marriage and residence as a means of establishing themselves as "Nyinba" in the community. At the first opportunity, they reorganize their families around male lines of descent, creating patriclan histories to reinforce their claim to Nyinba identity. Most dramatically, former slaves have begun to marry with both polyandry and patrilocal residence. The Nyinba case underscores again the cultural power of marriage and residence to create identity, difference, and inequality, both in domestic and social life.

Epilogue

What are the connections between marriage practice and other fields of social life? How does postmarital residence practice, together with other social processes, shape the meaning of marriage?

■ ■ ■

Focusing on the practice of marriage within diverse societies, this book has examined four cultures, each a classic case from the ethnographic record of a system that stands in striking contrast to our own. The primary analytical framework used to explicate not only the practice of marriage but its meaning as well is gender theory in American cultural anthropology. The gendered analysis of marriage in other societies yields insights into the differing meanings of marriage for husbands and wives—and causes us to reflect on the cultural constructions of our own.

Given the holistic perspective on culture, the anthropological analysis of marriage takes all of culture itself as critical context for its project. As the previous chapters have established, the analysis of marriage does not take the conjugal relationship as a creation of individual husbands and wives alone, based on their emotions and circumstances. Instead, the meaning of marriage relates to social processes that shape and constrain other arenas of social life. For each of the four societies, my analysis has explored the relationships among marriage and what one too often readily conceptualizes as separate domains (economy and polity, family and kinship, religion and ideology).

In this book, the significance of postmarital residence as a critical social process shaping marriage practice everywhere becomes apparent. In my field research on marriage in South China, I was continually struck by the power of postmarital residence in creating distinctively different experiences for husbands and wives in delayed transfer marriages. Indeed, from my viewpoint, it seemed that the relative position of the genders in that society could not be known without acknowledging the influence of customary postmarital residence practice: The delay in the transfer of a new wife to her husband's family's home—and sometimes a prolonged delay—greatly enhanced the domestic power and place of daughters in their own family, especially when they performed important work for their family in silk production.

Across diverse cultures, postmarital residence and kinship practices are social processes that place husbands and wives within already-established domestic hierarchies in families and households. In the case of delayed transfer marriage, it placed the wife (sooner or later) within her husband's family hierarchy, with profound consequences for the experience of marriage (and life) for both.

The !Kung San, described by anthropologists at a time when they still practiced hunting and gathering, lived in what has been widely considered a relatively egalitarian society, with little social stratification, few interest groups, and no political leaders. Marriage itself in this society was politics and created the most visible difference among men, that is, between bachelors and married men. Through marriage, men came to enjoy all the prerogatives of full adulthood, achieving position in both band and camp alongside other married men.

In that society, marriage established a relationship among several people: the bride, the groom, and the bride's parents. It organized economic relationships, among them a groom's obligation to hunt for his father-in-law during the period of brideservice. For brideservice, a new husband assumed uxorilocal residence, leaving his own family and band to take up residence with his young wife and her parents in their band. This residence practice clearly facilitated the work of brideservice by placing a husband within physical proximity to his father-in-law. Through brideservice, a husband established his marriage claim to the older man's daughter and supported the latter's political career with meat to redistribute. Uxorilocal residence and brideservice not only placed a husband in his father-in-law's camp and service but created a relationship of dependence, in which the younger man relied on the older to learn the hunting territory and resources of the band.

Beyond its links to the polity and economy, however, marriage with uxorilocal postmarital residence in !Kung San society shaped the dynamics of the conjugal relationship, tempering the domestic power of each partner with regard to the other. It reduced the possible adverse effects created by the disparity in ages of the husband and wife by establishing their residence alongside her parents. This created a domestic situation in which parents could continue to oversee the welfare of their young daughter and the behavior of her older husband to her. These protective effects of uxorilocal residence (within this society characterized by bilateral kinship) contrast especially with the effects of Chinese marriage, in a society with a very different kinship ideology and residence practice.

In agrarian Chinese society of the late nineteenth and early twentieth centuries, marriage with immediate patrilocal residence was the norm for most families (one exception being the area of delayed transfer marriage area in South China). Parents arranged marriages to accomplish a change in residence for their daughters, who were transferred from their natal family to their husband's. Daughters could not support their own parents with their labor or sons because both were claimed by their husband's family and line. For sons, marriage with patrilocal residence accomplished precisely the opposite result, retaining sons in co-residence with their parents. In removing a daughter from her natal family and placing her within her husband's family, marriage effectively isolated her from the protective custody of family and kin.

The chief objective of marriage in this patrilineal society was to continue the male line of descent into the future through sons and sons' sons. In this agrarian society, sons guaranteed the economic security of their parents in this life, as well as providing for them (through ancestor worship) in the next. Thus, given patrilineal kinship ideology and patrilocal residence practice, parents through the arrangement of the marriages of their children could create families and households built around the male line of descent—and reproduce it across the generations.

Residence in this context can readily be seen as strengthening the position of sons within natal families, while diminishing the standing of daughters, who were born to be recognized as but temporary members of the family. Within the homes of their husband, patrilocally resident wives had to assume inferior status positions within a domestic hierarchy of all other wives. The situation was made all the more complex in elite families in this class-based society by the practice of polygyny, whereby sons in elite families could marry multiple wives.

A wife's position as stranger in the home of her husband and his family necessitated the strategy of building a uterine family around her sons, thus securing their affections and loyalties, providing her with a base of emotional and economic support in the future. Each wife's uterine family, however, was poised to contest the claims of others. The isolating effects of patrilocal residence for a wife in large part shaped the contours of the experience of being "female" in Chinese society. The consolidating effects of residence on the position of sons within the Chinese family (enhanced by other cultural ideologies, as well) created the experience of being "male." This coupling of patrilineal kinship and patrilocal residence might seem at first to be re-created, but in reverse, in the case of the Iroquois.

Iroquois society of the nineteenth century was based not on plow agriculture but on horticulture and hunting and thus produced only partial stratification. Political authorities were titled male chiefs, who built their authority on prestige and the ability to gain consensus. Their power was negotiated, not absolute as it was among high state officials in China. They presided at councils over the affairs of the Iroquois nation, tribes, and clans, although their power was mediated by that of clan matriarchs, who enjoyed substantial domestic political power. Marriage practice was influenced by both matrilineal kinship and matrilocal residence, the combined effects of which were to retain daughters in the longhouse of their mothers and maternal aunts while dispersing sons into the longhouses of their wives. Families and households were built around a co-resident core of women related through the female line of descent. This situation tended to offset in part the privileged position of men in the public political arena, creating a more equitable relationship between men and women than was characteristic of agrarian societies.

Because women were the primary cultivators in this horticultural society, the twin effects of the social processes of kinship and residence enabled the division of labor, whereby daughters remained at home and farmed the land attached to the longhouse of their mothers. In contrast to the Chinese case, the change in residence with marriage did not remove sons from positions of responsibility in natal family, longhouse, lineage, and clan. Instead, Iroquois husbands retained positions of authority within the houses and descent lines of their mothers, inheriting chiefly titles from their maternal uncles and held responsibilities of guardianship within their mother's house. Kinship and residence practices, together with a division of labor in which both husbands and wives made important economic contributions, created a domestic situation characterized by modest gender hierarchy.

As in the case of Chinese society, Tibetan Nyinba society is also an agrarian society with both patrilineal kinship and patrilocal postmarital residence practice, but there the similarities end. Unlike China, neither land nor household is divided upon the death of the senior generation. Nyinba do not practice partible inheritance but live in households that can be described as corporate, with both land and house passing intact from one generation of brothers to the next. The loyalty nurtured among brothers in the uterine families of the Chinese is cultivated to a yet higher degree among the Nyinba. Here, brothers not only co-reside for life but share a common wife, manifesting from a cross-cultural perspective an extreme commitment to brotherly cooperation. Polyandry is one of the rarer marriage practices in the ethnographic record.

Given the constraints of alpine agriculture, including the scarcity of arable land, the demographic effects of the practice of polyandry could easily be taken as the continuing motive behind the arrangement of polyandrous marriages. Yet polyandry constitutes identity among the Nyinba (and other Tibetans) and is experienced as culture. Polyandry constitutes marriage for the Nyinba—much as delayed transfer marriage constitutes marriage for the Cantonese that I studied—and cannot be reduced to simple economic calculation from generation to generation. Polyandry is both the ideal and norm, and monogamy is practiced only by default, if only one son is born (or survives) in a generation. (Although monogamy can also be the outcome of household partitioning, it is deemed an unfortunate and un-Nyinba event by all.)

From a Western cultural perspective, the organization of family and household among the Nyinba may seem to privilege the position of wife, enhancing her status as the one wife of several husbands. Given the strong preference for males in this society, however, and the general devaluation of females and their work in the domestic division of labor, a wife does not enjoy the benefits of scarcity value. One outcome of the practice of polyandry is a perennial shortage of female labor in the household, a situation alleviated by slaves before their manumission. (Male slaves were further demeaned in the general domestic hierarchy by the requirement that they perform only work defined as female.) Thus, by the practice of patrilocal residence, a daughter was removed from her natal family and transferred as wife to the family and household of her husbands, who by the practice of polyandry were several (and related as brothers). There, she assumed a position at the bottom of a domestic hierarchy that favored males, further disadvantaged by a shortage of women in the household to perform female labor, created by the practice of marriage.

The analysis of marriage in these four societies also elicits for comparative purposes features of marriage practice in the United States and its greater cultural context. For example, bilateral kinship, a factor in !Kung San marriage, is also a component of marriages in the United States. However, the nuclear families built on this kinship system among the !Kung San and among Americans differ in the social processes that define them. In the !Kung San case, distinctive economic exchanges linked individual nuclear families, such as in brideservice. Other social processes, for example, the division of labor within those nuclear families between spouses, further distinguish !Kung San and American cases.

Analysis of the respective economic contributions of husbands and wives in all four societies also shows that they were set within the contrasting subsistence adaptations of each society. In the case of the Iroquois, for example, the differing contribution of the spouses to the longhouse economy can be compared with the "traditional" division of labor in American families, that is, the family wage ideology.

Americans represent diverse cultural origins and traditions. All of this diversity, however, is set within the context of shared cultural processes, ideologies, and institutions. Representing different ethnic and regional communities, individuals and members of families in the United States manifest different responses to these larger cultural forces, embodying different histories of accommodation, adaptation, and resistance to them. These differences include the practice(s) and meaning(s) of marriage in the contemporary era.

A backdrop to the experimentation and diversity of marriage within this postmodern era is a commonly perceived "traditional" time, when marriages were stable and adhered to a common form, based on shared cultural values. To some, that time and marriage practice mark the golden age of the American family, one evoked by contemporary politicians and others who call for a return to family values. That marriage practice (and family) continues to be relived through the endless reruns of television series and other media that enact and celebrate it. In this, it is once again created as memory and becomes a cultural touchstone, against which we measure our conformity (or departure from it) in the postmodern era.

In the traditional era, the division of labor (between husband-breadwinner and wife-homemaker) was enacted by marriage. This family was a product of a specific economy—the emerging industrial economy of the mid–nineteenth century, which required a mobile labor force. Mobility favored smaller, more nuclear families rather than extended ones, common to an earlier era and set in an economy based on family enterprise in shops and on farms. As family and home became separated from the workplace, social reformers championed the idea of a family wage, by which a husband's wage in the workplace was sufficient to support an unwaged wife at home.[1] This division of labor came to organize marriage and family life, ascribing different roles to husbands and wives, which in turn shaped the meaning of being "male" and "female" in this society.

The sleeker nuclear family of the industrial age was defined not only by economic forces but other social processes as well. A heightened cultural emphasis on individualism and independence, together with neolocal postmarital residence, created families that were increasingly isolated from the claims and obligations of an older generation. Marriages were arranged by young men and women themselves on the basis of love, which in a nuclear family based on neolocal residence did not threaten the authority and interests of their parents.[2]

Some scholars describe contemporary marriage practice(s) as the product of a postmodern era in which the very nature of kinship and gender is experienced as contested, ambiguous, and undecided. Marriage practices, and the families they create, seem increasingly experimental. Consider the blending of families as divorce and remarriage come to characterize the marital histories of many. Growing proportions of persons are marrying at later ages or choosing forms of nonmarriage—couplings and unions of various descriptions, including two or more partners, of one or more genders, sanctioned (or not) by diverse ideologies, religious and other.[3] Increasingly, a larger proportion of youth of marriageable age remains single and seems inclined never to marry at all. Some couples defy the constraints of marriage as defined by state and religious institutions and "marry" in unions prohibited by law and by religious belief.

This array of contemporary possibilities makes any remaining nostalgia for predictably uniform marriage and residence practices seem misplaced and prompts a number of questions: Will neolocal residence continue to be the dominant postmarital residence practice in this society, or will it be replaced by several (as yet unidentified) alternative patterns? In an era characterized by increasing experimentation in marriage (and nonmarriage) practices, even if neolocality were to remain the norm, what would be its influence on the division of labor between spouses and partners?

As already noted, one major outcome of the industrial revolution was the separation of home and work, and the ensuing creation of separate domestic and public spheres in which the division of labor was organized by the family wage ideology. As the workplace becomes increasingly reorganized as a result of both the rise of a new service-based economy and the development of new information technologies, more questions arise: Will those traditionally separate spheres be merged? How will change in the gendered division of labor affect the organization of parenting? In turn, how will shifts in both the practice and meaning of marriage and work affect gender itself, that is, what it means to be man, woman, husband, wife, or partner? Finally, given all of these changes, will postmarital (or postunion) residence practices continue to affect the relationship and hierarchy between (and among) the genders? These questions provide a starting point for understanding both the evolving nature of marriage in this postmodern era and its changing meaning with shifting residence and economic practices.

■
Notes

CHAPTER 1   MARRIAGE AS A CULTURAL PRACTICE

1. Questions about the interpretation of local marriage practices guided my ethnographic research, presented in Janice E. Stockard, *Daughters of the Canton Delta: Marriage Patterns and Economic Strategies in South China, 1860–1930* (Stanford, Calif.: Stanford University Press, 1989).

2. Franz Boas, considered to be the father of American anthropology, is credited with developing the concept of culture, which came to replace the nineteenth-century evolutionary assumption that only Europeans and Americans possessed culture (i.e., "civilization"). See George Stocking, "Franz Boas and the Concept of Culture in Historical Perspective," in *Race, Culture, and Evolution: Essays in the History of Anthropology,* ed. G. Stocking (Chicago: University of Chicago Press, 1982), pp. 195–233.

3. For information on the ethnographic methods employed by cultural anthropologists, see H. Russell Bernard, *Research Methods in Anthropology,* 2nd ed. (Thousand Oaks, Calif.: Sage, 1984), especially chapters 7 and 10, "Participant Observation" and "Unstructured and Semistructured Interviewing." Paul Rabinow provides a personal account of his fieldwork in his *Reflections on Fieldwork in Morocco* (Berkeley: University of California Press, 1977).

4. Stockard, "The Link between Sericulture and Marriage," chapter 8 in *Daughters of the Canton Delta,* describes silk-reeling labor and technology in South China.

5. Stockard, *Daughters of the Canton Delta,* especially chapter 1–3, establishes the difference between the practice of marriage and marriage resistance. See also Marjorie Topley, "Marriage Resistance in Rural Kwangtung," in *Women in Chinese*

Society, ed. M. Wolf and R. Witke (Stanford, Calif.: Stanford University Press, 1975), pp. 67–88.

6. The importance of reconceiving and rewriting interview questions during ethnographic fieldwork is described in Bernard, "Unstructured and Semistructured Interviewing," chapter 10 in *Research Methods in Anthropology,* as well as in Stockard, "The Right Question," appendix A in *Daughters of the Canton Delta.*

7. For an illuminating discussion of achieving an insider's perspective during fieldwork, see Lila Abu-Lughod, chapter 1 in her ethnography of the Bedouin in Egypt, *Veiled Sentiments: Honor and Poetry in a Bedouin Society* (Berkeley: University of California Press, 1986).

8. Stockard, *Daughters of the Canton Delta,* pp. 4–5.

9. The effects of changing technology in silk reeling on both marriage practice and the position of reelers themselves (within their natal and husband's family) are analyzed in Stockard, "The Link between Sericulture and Marriage," chapter 8 in *Daughters of the Canton Delta.*

10. Contemporary anthropologists use caution when describing societies as "traditional," which generally suggests premodern and/or precontact conditions. The portrayal of "traditional" societies is usually based on accounts of those societies as they were first described in the literature, that is, in the records and journals of travelers, colonial administrators, missionaries, and early anthropologists. The term *traditional,* therefore, suggests that a society is described before major changes have occurred as a result of contact with Western societies. Anthropologists employ the term only to describe a society during a specified historical era—as I do in this book. They seek to avoid suggesting that those societies were unchanging or untouched before their encounter with the West. For further discussion, see Eric Hobsbawm and Terrence Ranger, *The Invention of Tradition* (Cambridge: Cambridge University Press, 1983); and George Bond and Angela Gilliam, *Social Construction of the Past: Representation as Power* (London: Routledge, 1994).

The uncritical use of the term *traditional* can easily mislead readers to assume that people are presently still living the lives of the past, frozen in time. See also the discussion of the construction of the ethnographic present by anthropologists, for example, John Burton, "Shadows at Twilight: A Note on History and the Ethnographic Present," *Proceedings of the American Philosophical Society* 132 (1988): 420–33.

11. Gendered analyses of marriage elucidating the differing experiences and meanings for husbands and wives include Jane Collier, *Marriage and Inequality in Classless Societies* (Stanford, Calif.: Stanford University Press, 1988); and Verena Martinez-Alier, *Marriage, Class, and Colour in Nineteenth-Century Cuba: A Study of Racial Attitudes and Sexual Values in a Slave Society* (Cambridge: Cambridge University Press, 1974).

12. For a discussion of the co-construction of the fields of kinship and gender, see Sylvia Yanagisako and Jane Collier, "Toward a Unified Analysis of Gender and Kinship," in *Gender and Kinship: Essays toward a Unified Analysis,* ed. J. Collier and S. Yanagisako (Stanford, Calif.: Stanford University Press, 1987), pp. 1–50.

13. For a discussion of anthropological approaches to the study of child socialization and cultural learning, also referred to as cultural transmission, see George Spindler, ed., *Education and Cultural Process: Anthropological Approaches,* 3rd ed. (Prospect Heights, Ill.: Waveland, 1997).

14. Ethnographies of ethnic groups within the United States practicing other forms of postmarital residence include Carol Stack, *All Our Kin: Strategies for Survival in a Black Community* (New York: Harper Row, 1974); and Ruth Underhill, *The Navahos* (Norman: University of Oklahoma Press, 1956).
15. Examples of anthropological works focusing on the relationship between marriage and economy include Judith Brown, "Economic Organization and the Position of Women among the Iroquois," *Ethnohistory* 17 (1970): 151–67; and Marjorie Shostak, *Nisa: The Life and Words of a !Kung Woman* (New York: Random House, 1981).
16. For works employing economic and ecological anthropological approaches, see, for example, Marvin Harris, *Cows, Pigs, Wars, and Witches: The Riddles of Culture* (New York: Random House, 1975); and Marshall Sahlins, "Culture and Environment: The Study of Cultural Ecology," in *Theory in Anthropology*, ed. R. Manners and D. Kaplan (New York: Aldine), pp. 367–73.
17. For examples of neo-Marxist writing in anthropology, see Claude Meillassoux, *Maidens, Meal, and Money* (New York: Cambridge University Press, 1981); and Maurice Godelier, *Marxist Perspectives in Anthropology* (Cambridge: Cambridge University Press, 1977).
18. The traditions of British structuralism are exemplified in the writings of Paul Bohannan, *Justice and Judgement among the Tiv* (London: Oxford University Press, 1957); and Maurice Freedman, *Chinese Lineage and Society* (London: London School of Economics, 1966).
19. Pierre Bourdieu's theory of practice is presented in his *Outlines of a Theory of Practice* (Cambridge: Cambridge University Press, 1977).
20. Their theoretical approach to the study of gender in society is introduced in Yanagisako and Collier, "Toward a Unified Analysis of Gender and Kinship."
21. In the field of kinship studies, the subject of postmarital residence practice has been controversial. Historically, although anthropologists could agree that residence is the outcome of rules of recruitment and succession, they could not agree on whether residence played a determining role in domestic group formation. See Paul Bohannan, *Social Anthropology* (New York: Holt, Rinehart and Winston, 1963).

     For recent treatments of postmarital residence, see Stevan Harrell, *Human Families* (Boulder, Colo.: Westview, 1997); Robert McC.Netting, Richard R. Wilk, and Eric J. Arnould, eds. *Households: Comparative and Historical Studies of the Domestic Group* (Berkeley: University of California Press, 1984); and Michel Verdon, *Rethinking Households: An Atomistic Perspective on European Living Arrangements* (London: Routledge, 1998).

CHAPTER 2   MARRIAGE AMONG THE !KUNG SAN OF SOUTHERN AFRICA

1. Elizabeth Marshall Thomas, *The Harmless People*, 2nd ed. (New York: Random House, 1989), p. 154.
2. The San languages are classified as belonging to a language family known as "Click" or Khoisan and characterized by click sounds produced when, during the intake of air, the tongue is drawn sharply away from the roof of the mouth. Four different clicks are used by the !Kung San. The one indicated by the exclamation point preceding the "k" in their name is an alveopalatal click.
3. The !Kung San have of course been undergoing change throughout their long history, encountering indigenous peoples practicing other kinds of subsistence

adaptations, including pastoralists and horticulturists. These peoples have steadily encroached on !Kung San traditional territories, erecting fences and boundaries that have brought a virtual end to the !Kung San's traditional mode of subsistence based on hunting and gathering. In what is now Botswana, the !Kung San have experienced change primarily as a result of "sedentarism," or settling down to take up a lifestyle like their neighbors, based on simple farming or herding. Change for the !Kung San in what is now Namibia has been more cataclysmic; until 1990 they lived under South African rule, suffering the effects of life under apartheid in the 1970s and 1980s.

Change within !Kung San society is addressed in Robert Gordon, *The Bushman Myth: The Making of a Namibian Underclass* (Boulder, Colo.: Westview, 1992); John Yellen, "The Transformation of the Kalahari !Kung," *Scientific American* 262, no. 4 (1990): 96–105; Patricia Draper, "!Kung Women: Contrasts in Sexual Egalitarianism in Foraging and Sedentary Contexts," in *Toward an Anthropology of Women,* ed. Rayna Reiter (New York: Monthly Review Press, 1975); and Richard B. Lee, *The Dobe Ju/'hoansi,* 2nd ed. (New York: Harcourt Brace, 1993). See also the John Marshall films *N!ai: The Story of a !Kung Woman* (Boston: Documentary Educational Resources, 1980), *Pull Ourselves Up or Die* (Cambridge, MA: DER, 1985), and *!Kung San Resettlement* (DER, 1988).

4. The primary ethnographic sources used for the analysis of the !Kung San include Richard B. Lee and Irven Devore, eds., *Kalahari Hunter-Gatherers* (Cambridge, Mass.: Harvard University Press, 1976); Richard B. Lee, *The !Kung San: Men, Women, and Work in a Foraging Society* (Cambridge: Cambridge University Press, 1979); Lee, *The Dobe Ju/'hoansi;* Thomas, *The Harmless People;* Shostak, *Nisa;* Richard Katz, *Boiling Energy: Community Healing among the Kalahari Kung* (Cambridge, Mass.: Harvard University Press, 1982); and Alan Barnard, *Hunters and Herders of Southern Africa: A Comparative Ethnography of Khoisan Peoples* (Cambridge: Cambridge University Press, 1992). For a comparative perspective on the !Kung San, see also Jared Diamond, *Guns, Germs, and Steel: The Fates of Human Societies* (New York: Norton, 1997). Film resources are equally rich, the best including John Marshall's *The Hunters* (Cambridge, MA: DER, 1957), *!Kung Bushmen Hunting Equipment, Playing with Scorpions* (Cambridge, MA: DER, 1972), *A Rite of Passage* (Cambridge, MA: DER, 1972), *The Meat Fight* (Cambridge, MA: DER, 1974), and *N!ai: The Story of a !Kung Woman* (Boston: Documentary Educational Resources, 1980).

5. The best ethnographic sources on marriage and brideservice among the !Kung San are Thomas, *The Harmless People;* and Shostak, *Nisa.*

6. The present analysis of the relationships created by brideservice follows the model for understanding brideservice cross-culturally, developed by Collier in *Marriage and Inequality in Classless Societies.*

7. For more information on the general organization of societies in which brideservice is practiced—what are variously called band, foraging, hunter-gatherer, and egalitarian societies—see Elman Service, *Primitive Social Organization: An Evolutionary Perspective* (New York: Random House, 1962); Morton Fried, *The Evolution of Political Society* (New York: Random House, 1967); and Claude Meillassoux, "From Reproduction to Production," *Economy and Society* 1 (1972): 83–105.

8. For further information on the nature of egalitarian societies, see Michelle Z. Rosaldo, "Woman, Culture, and Society: A Theoretical Overview," in *Woman, Culture, and Society,* ed. M. Rosaldo and L. Lamphere (Stanford, Calif.: Stanford University Press, 1974); Fried, *The Evolution of Political Society;* Eleanor Leacock,

"Women's Status in Egalitarian Society: Implications for Social Evolution," *Current Anthropology* 9, no. 2 (1978): 247–75; and Ernestine Friedl, *Women and Men: An Anthropologist's View* (New York: Holt, Rinehart and Winston, 1975; reprint, Prospect Heights, Ill.: Waveland Press, 1984). See also Jane Collier and Michelle Z. Rosaldo, "Politics and Gender in Simple Societies," in *Sexual Meanings,* ed. S. Ortner and H. Whitehead (New York: Cambridge University Press, 1981), pp. 275–329; Richard B. Lee, "Politics, Sexual and Nonsexual, in an Egalitarian Society: The !Kung San," in *Social Inequality,* ed. G. Berreman (New York: Academic Press, 1981), pp. 83–101; and Elizabeth Marshall Thomas, *Reindeer Moon* (Boston: Houghton Mifflin, 1987), a fictionalized account of a northern European egalitarian band of hunters and gatherers, informed by her ethnographic observations of the !Kung San and Australian indigenous peoples.

9. I describe the !Kung San way of life and marriage in the present tense because the bulk of the ethnographic record documenting their traditional hunting-and-gathering subsistence was compiled relatively recently, in the 1950s through the 1970s. (For information on the !Kung after the demise of hunting and gathering, see note 3 in this chapter.) For the historical Chinese and Iroquois ethnographic cases in chapters 3 and 4, I use the past tense in my discussion. For the Nyinba discussed in chapter 5, I use the present tense. The descriptions of the Nyinba date primarily from the 1980s and 1990s, with a few references to historical eras. See also chapter 1, note 10, for a discussion of the construction of "traditional" societies.

10. See Lee, *The !Kung San;* and Shostak, *Nisa,* for more information on the subsistence contributions of men and women.

11. For further discussion on kinship among the !Kung San, see Lorna Marshall, *The !Kung of Nyae Nyae* (Cambridge, Mass.: Harvard University Press, 1976). On kinship in the United States, see David Schneider, *American Kinship: A Cultural Account,* 2nd ed. (Chicago: University of Chicago Press, 1980).

12. See Lorna Marshall, "Sharing, Talking, and Giving: Relief of Social Tensions among the !Kung," in *Kalahari Hunter-Gatherers,* ed. R. Lee and I. DeVore (Cambridge, Mass.: Harvard University Press, 1976), p. 364.

13. On reciprocity, see Thomas, *The Harmless People;* and Marshall, "Sharing, Talking, and Giving," and *The !Kung of Nyae Nyae.* See also Shostak, *Nisa,* for descriptions of techniques to encourage sharing and discourage "stingy" behavior, and Richard B. Lee, "Eating Christmas in the Kalahari," included as an appendix in *The Dobe Ju/'Hoansi.*

14. Lee, *The Dobe Ju/'hoansi,* p. 55.

15. See Rosaldo, "Woman, Culture, and Society: A Theoretical Overview."

16. See Rosaldo, "Woman, Culture, and Society: A Theoretical Overview."

17. See Collier, *Marriage and Inequality in Classless Societies,* pp. 15–70, for an analysis of Comanche brideservice.

18. For more information, visually presented, see John Marshall's *A Rite of Passage* (Cambridge, MA: DER, 1972).

19. For further discussion on men and parity in egalitarian societies, see Collier, *Marriage and Inequality in Classless Societies;* Fried, *The Evolution of Political Society;* and Collier and Rosaldo, "Politics and Gender in Simple Societies."

20. The most informative sources on childhood and sexuality are provided in Patricia Draper, "Social and Economic Constraints on Child Life among the !Kung," in *Kalahari Hunter-Gatherers,* ed. R. Lee and I. DeVore, pp. 199–217; Shostak, *Nisa;* and Marshall, *The !Kung of Nyae Nyae.*

21. For more information on conflict and dispute resolution, see especially Lee, *The !Kung San* and "Politics, Sexual and Nonsexual, in an Egalitarian Society." Films that focus on conflict over meat and sex, respectively, include John Marshall's *The Meat Fight* (Cambridge, MA: DER, 1974) and *An Argument about a Marriage*.

CHAPTER 3   MARRIAGE IN TRADITIONAL CHINESE SOCIETY

1. Justus Doolittle, *Social Life of the Chinese* (New York: Harper, 1865), 1:75.
2. As used in this chapter, "traditional" Chinese society describes late imperial times, primarily the nineteenth and early twentieth centuries, prior to the establishment of the People's Republic of China in 1949.
3. Primary sources for ethnographic information on marriage in traditional Chinese society include Arthur Wolf, *Marriage and Adoption in China, 1845–1945* (Stanford, Calif.: Stanford University Press, 1972); Margery Wolf, *Women and the Family in Rural Taiwan* (Stanford, Calif.: Stanford University Press, 1972); Rubie Watson, and Patricia Ebrey, eds., *Marriage and Inequality in Chinese Society* (Berkeley: University of California Press, 1991); Martin C. Yang, *A Chinese Village* (New York: Columbia University Press, 1945); and Stockard, *Daughters of the Canton Delta*.
4. For a discussion of the organization features of agrarian societies, see Gerhard Lenski, *Power and Privilege* (New York: McGraw Hill, 1966); and Fried, *The Evolution of Political Society*.
5. For discussion of the organization and hierarchy of classes in Chinese society, see G. William Skinner, "Mobility Strategies in Late Imperial China," in *Regional Analysis,* ed. C. Smith, vol. 1 (New York: Academic Press, 1976); Ho Ping-ti, *The Ladder of Success in Imperial China: Aspects of Social Mobility, 1368–1911* (New York: Columbia University Press, 1962); Edwin Moise, "Downward Social Mobility in Pre-Revolutionary China," *Modern China* 3 (1977): 3–32; James L. Watson, "Transactions in People: The Chinese Market in Slaves, Servants, and Heirs," in *Asian and African Systems of Slavery,* ed. J.L. Watson (Oxford: Basil Blackwell, 1980); Rubie Watson, *Inequality among Brothers: Class and Kinship in South China* (Cambridge: Cambridge University Press, 1985); and R. Watson and P. Ebrey, eds., *Marriage and Inequality in Class Society.*
6. See Lenski, *Power and Privilege;* Carol Ember, "The Relative Decline in Women's Contribution to Agriculture with Intensification," *American Anthropologist* 85 (1983): 285–304; and Ester Boserup, *Woman's Role in Economic Development* (New York: St. Martin's Press, 1970).
7. For discussion, see Peggy Sanday, "Female Status in the Public Domain," in *Woman, Culture, and Society,* ed. M. Rosaldo and L. Lamphere (Stanford, Calif.: Stanford University Press, 1974), pp. 189–206; William T. Divale and Marvin Harris, "Population, Warfare, and the Male Supremacist Complex," *American Anthropologist* 78 (1976): 521–38; and Naomi Quinn, "Anthropological Studies on Women's Status," *Annual Review of Anthropology* 6 (1977): 189–90.
8. See Diamond, *Guns, Germs, and Steel,* pp. 104–13.
9. On horticulture and the division of labor, see Friedl, *Women and Men.*
10. See Rosaldo, "Woman, Culture, and Society: A Theoretical Overview"; Draper, "!Kung Women"; and Sanday, "Female Status in the Public Domain."
11. On the position of women in state societies, see Sherry Ortner, "The Virgin and the State," *Feminist Studies* 4, no. 3 (1978): 19–35, and "Gender Hegemonies," in *Making Gender: The Politics and Erotics of Culture,* ed. S. Ortner (Boston: Beacon Press,

1996), pp. 139–72; and Irene Silverblatt, "Interpreting Women in States: New Feminist Ethnohistories," in *Gender at the Crossroads,* ed. M. di Leonardo (Berkeley: University of California Press, 1991), pp. 140–74.

12. On the practice of footbinding, see Dorothy Ko, "The Body as Attire: The Shifting Meanings of Footbinding in Seventeenth Century China," in her *Teachers of the Inner Chambers* (Stanford, Calif.: Stanford University Press, 1994); Christine Turner, "Locating Footbinding: Variations across Class and Space in Nineteenth and Early Twentieth Century China," *Journal of Historical Sociology* 10, no. 4 (1997): 444–79; Susan Mann, *Precious Records: Women in China's Long Eighteenth Century* (Stanford, Calif.: Stanford University Press, 1997); and Howard Levy, *Chinese Footbinding* (Tokyo: Weatherhill, 1966).

13. For a discussion of the Chinese male descent line and male ancestor worship, see A. Wolf, *Marriage and Adoption in Chinese Society;* and Maurice Freedman, "Ancestor Worship: Two Facets of the Chinese Case," in *Social Organization,* ed. M. Freedman (Chicago: University of Chicago Press, 1967), pp. 85–103.

14. Sources on the Chinese lineage include Freedman, *Chinese Lineage and Society;* A. Wolf, *Marriage and Adoption in Chinese Society;* R. Watson, *Inequality among Brothers;* and James L. Watson, *Emigration and the Chinese Lineage: The Mans in Hong Kong and London* (Berkeley: University of California Press, 1975).

15. On women's place in male descent lines, see A. Wolf, *Marriage and Adoption in Chinese Society;* and Stockard, *Daughters of the Canton Delta.*

16. See Stockard, *Daughters of the Canton Delta;* and Topley, "Marriage Resistance in Rural Kwangtung," for further discussion of the unorthodox marriage practices in South China. For a description of delayed transfer marriage as it was practiced within an historical indigenous population (non-Han Chinese) in Taiwan, see John Shepherd, *Marriage and Mandatory Abortion among the Seventeenth Century Siraya* (N.p.: American Ethnological Society, 1995).

17. The practice of spirit marriage in Chinese society is analyzed in Arthur Wolf, "Gods, Ghosts, and Ancestors," in *Religion and Ritual in Chinese Society,* ed. A. Wolf (Stanford, Calif.: Stanford University Press, 1974), pp. 131–82; and Stockard, *Daughters of the Canton Delta.*

18. See Stockard, *Daughters of the Canton Delta,* chapters 1–5.

19. This analysis of the meaning of marriage for a daughter in traditional Chinese society is based on Stockard, *Daughters of the Canton Delta.*

20. For a complete discussion of the uterine family, see M. Wolf, *Women and the Family in Rural Taiwan.*

21. Maidservants, concubines, and secondary marriage are discussed in Rubie Watson, "Wives, Concubines, and Maids: Servitude and Kinship in the Hong Kong Region, 1900–1940," in *Marriage and Inequality in Chinese Society,* ed. R. Watson and P. Ebrey, pp. 231–55; Maria Jaschok, *Concubines and Bondservants* (Hong Kong: Oxford, 1988); Stockard, *Daughters of the Canton Delta;* and Janice E. Stockard, "Reeling Silk and Identity in Natal Homes: Residence, Labor, and the Production of Daughters in South China" (paper presented at the 99th Annual Meeting of the American Anthropological Association, November 2000).

CHAPTER 4 MARRIAGE AMONG THE HISTORICAL IROQUOIS

1. Lewis Henry Morgan, *League of the Ho-de-no-sau-nee, Iroquois* (1851; reprint, New York: Corinth Press, 1962), pp. 321–22.

2. For a discussion of the place of matrilineal societies cross-culturally, see David Schneider and Kathleen Gough, eds., *Matrilineal Kinship* (Berkeley: University of California Press, 1961), especially David Schneider, "The Distinctive Features of Matrilineal Descent Groups," pp. 1–29.

3. In addition to Morgan's *League of the Ho-de-no-sau-nee, or Iroquois,* ethnographic sources on the Iroquois include Michael K. Foster, Jack Campisi, and Marianne Mithun, eds., *Extending the Rafters: Interdisciplinary Approaches to Iroquoian Studies* (New York: State University of New York); Thomas Abler, "Iroquois: The Tree of Peace and the War Kettle," in *Portraits of Culture,* ed. M. Ember, C. Ember, and D. Levinson (Englewood Cliffs, N.J.: Prentice-Hall, 1994), pp. 33–66, and "Moiety Exogamy and the Seneca: Evidence from Buffalo Creek," *Anthropological Quarterly* 44 (1971): 211–22; Elizabeth Tooker, "The League of the Iroquois: Its History, Politics, and Ritual," in *Handbook of North American Indians,* vol. 15, *Northeast,* ed. B. Trigger (Washington, D.C.: Smithsonian Institution, 1978), pp. 418–41; Anthony Wallace, *The Death and Rebirth of the Seneca* (New York: Knopf, 1970); William N. Fenton, ed., *Parker on the Iroquois* (New York: Syracuse University Press, 1968); William N. Fenton, *The Great Law and the Longhouse: A Political History of the Iroquois Confederacy* (Norman: University of Oklahoma Press, 1998); W. G. Spittal, *Iroquois Women: An Anthology* (Ontario: Iroqrafts, 1990); and Laura F. Klein and Lillian Ackerman, eds., *Women and Power in Native North America* (Norman: University of Oklahoma Press, 1995).

4. Morgan's contributions to both Iroquois ethnography and the field of kinship studies are discussed in Thomas Trautmann, *Lewis Henry Morgan and the Invention of Kinship* (Berkeley: University of California Press, 1987); and Rosalind Coward, *Patriarchal Precedents: Sexuality and Social Relations* (London: Routledge, 1983).

5. See in particular the preface to Friedrich Engels, *The Origin of the Family, Private Property and the State, in the Light of the Researches of Lewis H. Morgan* (1891; reprint, New York: International Publishers, 1942), pp. 5–18, in which Engels discusses Morgan's contribution to the development of Karl Marx's thought on the origin of the family.

6. For a discussion of the origins of complex kinship systems, see Fried, *The Evolution of Political Society;* Meillassoux, "From Reproduction to Production"; Friedl, *Women and Men;* and Carol Ember, Melvin Ember, and Burton Pasternak, "On the Development of Unilineal Descent," *Journal of Anthropological Research* 30 (1974): 69–94.

7. Birth outside of marriage in matrilineal societies did not jeopardize a child's identity because birth itself established the child's relationship to mother's descent line and clan. Such a child would be socially disadvantaged without a recognized father, but its status as a child belonging to its mother's group was not at stake. This contrasts with the position of a child born out of wedlock in patrilineal societies, whereby marriage or recognition by a father is required to establish a child's identity and claims to privileges in the father's line and group.

8. See Judith Stacey, *Brave New Families: Stories of Domestic Upheaval in Late Twentieth Century America* (New York: Basic Books: 1990); Martha May, "The Historical Problem of the Family Wage," *Feminist Studies* 8, no. 2 (1982): 399–424; and Jean Potuchek, *Who Supports the Family? Gender and Breadwinning in Dual-Earner Marriages* (Stanford, Calif.: Stanford University Press, 1997). See also Lillian Rubin, *Worlds of Pain: Life in the Working-Class Family* (New York: Basic

Books, 1976), which provides a cultural and gendered description of marriage practice and ideology in white working-class families in the 1970s.

9. Michelle Rosaldo defines and critiques, respectively, her model of the universal division of social space into opposed "domestic" and "public" spheres in "Woman, Culture, and Society: A Theoretical Overview" and "The Use and Abuse of Anthropology: Reflections on Feminism and Cross-Cultural Understanding," *Signs* 5, no. 3 (1980): 389–417.

10. See Joan Bamberger, "The Myth of Matriarchy," in *Women, Culture, and Society,* ed. M. Rosaldo and L. Lamphere (Stanford, Calif.: Stanford University Press, 1974); and Coward, *Patriarchal Precedents.*

11. Sources on the complexities of Iroquois kinship include Morgan, *League of the Ho-de-no-sau-nee, Iroquois*; Abler, "Moiety Exogamy and the Seneca" and "Iroquois"; and Trautmann, *Lewis Henry Morgan and the Invention of Kinship.* One feature of the Iroquois kinship system is what anthropologists call *moiety* organization, or the division of all clans into two separate groups or sides. Usually, moieties are important in the organization of marriage, in that a person is required to marry someone not only from a different clan but from the other moiety as well. However, the significance of moieties in the arrangement of Iroquois marriage is not clear. See Abler, "Moiety Exogamy and the Seneca."

12. Research that illuminates the relationship between spouses in Iroquois society include Joy Bilharz, "First among Equals? The Changing Status of Seneca Women," in *Women and Power in Native North America,* ed. L. F. Klein and L. Ackerman (Norman: University of Oklahoma Press, 1995), pp. 75–100; Elizabeth Tooker, "Women in Iroquois Society," in *Extending the Rafters: Interdisciplinary Approaches to Iroquoian Studies,* ed. M. Foster, J. Campisi, and M. Mithun (Albany: State University of New York, 1984), pp. 109–23; and Brown, "Economic Organization and the Position of Women among the Iroquois."

13. See especially Bronislaw Malinowski, *The Sexual Life of Savages in North-Western Melanesia* (1929; reprint, Boston: Beacon, 1987); and Annette Weiner, *The Trobrianders of Papua New Guinea* (New York: Holt, Rinehart and Winston, 1988), and *Women of Value, Men of Renown* (Austin: University of Texas, 1976).

14. For discussion of the brother-sister bond in Trobriand society, see Annette Weiner, "Trobriand Kinship from Another View: The Reproductive Power of Women and Men," *Man* 14 (1978): 328–48. The special emphasis given the mother-daughter bond in another matrilineal society, that among the Minangkabau, is analyzed in Evelyn Blackwood, *Webs of Power: Women, Kin, and Community in a Sumatran Village* (New York: Rowman and Littlefield, 2000). General discussion and analysis of the relationship of brothers and sisters in matrilineal societies can be found in Schneider and Gough, eds., *Matrilineal Kinship.*

15. The nature of marriage in matrilineal societies is described best in Malinowski, *The Sexual Life of Savages;* Weiner, *The Trobrianders of Papua New Guinea* and *Women of Value, Men of Renown;* Blackwood, *Webs of Power;* and Schneider and Gough, eds., *Matrilineal Kinship.*

CHAPTER 5   MARRIAGE AMONG TIBETANS: THE NYINBA OF NEPAL

1. Nancy Levine, *The Dynamics of Polyandry: Kinship, Domesticity, and Population on the Tibetan Border* (Chicago: University of Chicago Press, 1988), p. 5.

2. Ethnographic sources on Tibetan and Nyinba polyandry include Melvyn Goldstein, "Stratification, Polyandry, and Family Structure in Central Tibet," *Southwestern Journal of Anthropology* 27 (1971): 64–74, "Fraternal Polyandry and Fertility in a High Himalayan Valley in Northwest Nepal," *Human Ecology* 4 (1976): 423–33, and "When Brothers Share a Wife," *Natural History,* March 1987, pp. 39–48; and Nancy Levine, "Nyinba Polyandry and the Allocation of Paternity," *Journal of Comparative Family Studies* 11 (1980): 283–98, "Perspectives on Love: Morality and Affect in Nyinba Interpersonal Relationships," in *Culture and Morality: Essays in Honor of Christoph von Fürer-Haimendorf,* ed. A. C. Mayer (Delhi: Oxford University Press, 1981), and *The Dynamics of Polyandry.* Comparative treatments of polyandry include Jack Goody, *The Oriental, the Ancient, and the Primitive: Systems of Marriage and the Family in the Pre-Industrial Societies of Eurasia* (Cambridge: Cambridge University Press, 1985); and Gerald Berreman, "Himalayan Polyandry and the Domestic Cycle," *American Ethnologist* 2 (1975): 127–38, and "Polyandry: Exotic Custom vs. Analytic Concept," *Journal of Comparative Family Studies* 11 (1980): 377–83. General historical sources include R. A. Stein, *Tibetan Civilization* (Stanford, Calif.: Stanford University Press, 1972); Prince Peter of Greece and Denmark, "The Tibetan Family System," in *Comparative Family Systems,* ed. M. F. Nimkoff (Boston: Houghton Mifflin, 1965), pp. 192–208, and *A Study of Polyandry* (The Hague: n.p., 1963); Charles Bell, *The People of Tibet* (Oxford: Clarendon Press, 1928); Hugh Richardson, *High Peaks, Pure Earth: Collected Writings on Tibetan History and Culture* (London: Serindia, 1998); and Melvyn Goldstein, *A History of Modern Tibet, 1913–1951* (Berkeley: University of California Press, 1989).
3. See Coward's discussion in *Patriarchal Precedents,* chapters 1 and 2.
4. See Goldstein, "Stratification, Polyandry, and Family Structure in Central Tibet," "Fraternal Polyandry and Fertility in a High Himalayan Valley in Northwest Nepal," and "When Brothers Share a Wife"; and Levine, "Nyinba Polyandry and the Allocation of Paternity," "Perspectives on Love," and *The Dynamics of Polyandry.* The Nyinba also have hereditary clans of Buddhist lamas, on which there is little ethnographic information.
5. Refer to Carroll Dunham, "A Marriage in Shambhala," for information on Nyinba marriage customs. 1986 *Geo* (Paris, France), Vol. 94: 17–21.
6. For an excellent discussion of the internal family and household dynamics created by polyandry, see Levine, *The Dynamics of Polyandry;* and Nancy Levine and Joan Silk, "Why Polyandry Fails: Sources of Instability in Polyandrous Marriages," *Current Anthropology* 38, no. 3 (1997): 375–88.
7. See Dunham, "A Marriage in Shambhala," for an ethnographic description of a Nyinba wedding. 1986 *Geo* (Paris, France), Vol. 94: 17–21.
8. See Levine, *The Dynamics of Polyandry,* for discussion of paternity and inheritance among the Nyinba, chapter 7.
9. For a discussion of Nyinba slavery, see Nancy Levine, "Opposition and Interdependence: Demographic and Economic Perspectives on Nyinba Slavery," in *Asian and African Systems of Slavery,* ed. J. L. Watson (Berkeley: University of California Press, 1980): 195–222.
10. For a discussion of other societies with systems of slavery in which marriage itself creates and sustains inequality, see J. L. Watson, "Transactions in People"; and Martinez-Alier, *Marriage, Class and Colour in Nineteenth Century Cuba.*

EPILOGUE

1. May, "The Historical Problem of the Family Wage," discusses the origin of the family wage. Joan Acker, "Class, Gender, and the Relations of Distribution," *Signs* 13, no. 3 (1988): 473–97, addresses the effect of the family wage ideology on family and state policy. For an ethnographic description of the way in which the family wage ideology shaped gendered meanings of marriage in the working class in the 1970s, see Rubin, *Worlds of Pain*. For an analysis of the legacy of that ideology in contemporary times (and its effect on gender), see Potuchek, *Who Supports the Family?*; and Stacey, *Brave New Families*. Anthropological analyses of the families created by the family wage ideology include Schneider, *American Kinship*; and Rayna Rapp, "Family and Class in Contemporary America: Notes toward an Understanding of Ideology," in *Rethinking the Family: Some Feminist Questions*, ed. B. Thorne, with M. Yalom (New York: Longman, 1982), pp. 168–87.

2. The effects of industrialization and modernization on marriage, family, kinship, and gender are analyzed in William Goode, *World Revolution and Family Patterns* (New York: Free Press, 1970). Goode predicted a "convergence" cross-culturally on the American nuclear family model as other societies underwent these same changes. Discussion by scholars of the success of Goode's convergence theory to predict social change in various developing societies is found in *World Revolution and Family Patterns*, pp. 1–86. Deborah Davis and Stevan Harrell, *Chinese Families in the Post-Mao Era* (Berkeley: University of California Press, 1993), analyzes the ability of Goode's theory to predict change specifically in contemporary China.

3. For a general introduction to diversity in family, kinship, and marriage relations in the contemporary era, see Stacey, *Brave New Families*. See also ethnographies and analyses by anthropologists, including Kath Weston, *Families We Choose: Lesbians, Gays, Kinship* (New York: Columbia University Press, 1991); Ellen Lewin, *Lesbian Mothers* (Ithaca: Cornell University Press, 1993); and Gilbert Herdt, *Gay Culture in America* (Boston: Beacon Press, 1992). For discussion of changing reproductive technologies and issues, see Faye Ginsburg and Rayna Rapp, *Conceiving the New World Order: The Global Politics of Reproduction* (Berkeley: University of California Press, 1995).

References

Abler, Thomas S. 1994. "Iroquois: The Tree of Peace and the War Kettle." In *Portraits of Culture*, ed. M. Ember, C. Ember, and D. Levinson, pp. 33–66. Englewood Cliffs, N.J.: Prentice-Hall.

———. 1971. "Moiety Exogamy and the Seneca: Evidence from Buffalo Creek." *Anthropological Quarterly* 44:211–22.

Abu-Lughod, Lila. 1986. *Veiled Sentiments: Honor and Poetry in a Bedouin Society*. Berkeley: University of California Press.

Acker, Joan. 1988. "Class, Gender, and the Relations of Distribution." *Signs* 13, no. 3:473–97.

Bamberger, Joan. 1974. "The Myth of Matriarchy." In *Woman, Culture, and Society*, ed. M. Rosaldo and L. Lamphere, pp. 263–80. Stanford, Calif.: Stanford University Press.

Barnard, Alan. 1992. Hunters and Herders of Southern Africa: A Comparative Ethnography of Khoisan Peoples. Cambridge: Cambridge University Press.

Bell, Charles. 1928. *The People of Tibet*. Oxford: Clarendon Press.

Bernard, H. Russell. 1984. *Research Methods in Anthropology*, 2nd ed. Thousand Oaks, Calif.: Sage.

Berreman, Gerald. 1975. "Himalayan Polyandry and the Domestic Cycle." *American Ethnologist* 2:127–38.

———. 1980. "Polyandry: Exotic Custom vs. Analytic Concept." *Journal of Comparative Family Studies* 11:377–83.

Bilharz, Joy. 1995. "First among Equals? The Changing Status of Seneca Women." In *Women and Power in Native North America,* ed. L. F. Klein and L. A. Ackerman, pp. 75–100. Norman: University of Oklahoma Press.

Blackwood, Evelyn. 2000. *Webs of Power: Women, Kin, and Community in a Sumatran Village.* New York: Rowman and Littlefield.

Bohannan, Paul. 1957. *Justice and Judgement among the Tiv.* London: Oxford University Press.

———. 1963. *Social Anthropology.* New York: Holt, Rinehart and Winston.

Bond, George, and Angela Gilliam. 1994. *Social Construction of the Past: Representation as Power.* London: Routledge.

Boserup, Ester. 1970. *Woman's Role in Economic Development.* New York: St. Martin's Press.

Bourdieu, Pierre. 1977. *Outline of a Theory of Practice.* Cambridge: Cambridge University Press.

Brown, Judith. 1970. "Economic Organization and the Position of Women among the Iroquois." *Ethnohistory* 17:151–67.

Burton, John. 1988. "Shadows at Twilight: A Note on History and the Ethnographic Present." *Proceedings of the American Philosophical Society* 132:420–33.

Collier, Jane. 1988. *Marriage and Inequality in Classless Societies.* Stanford, Calif.: Stanford University Press.

Collier, Jane, and Michelle Z. Rosaldo. 1981. "Politics and Gender in Simple Societies." In *Sexual Meanings,* ed. S. Ortner and H. Whitehead, pp. 275–329. New York: Cambridge University Press.

Coward, Rosalind. 1983. *Patriarchal Precedents: Sexuality and Social Relations.* London: Routledge.

Davis, Deborah, and Stevan Harrell, eds. 1993. *Chinese Families in the Post-Mao Era.* Berkeley: University of California Press.

Diamond, Jared. 1997. *Guns, Germs, and Steel: The Fates of Human Societies.* New York: Norton.

Divale, William T., and Marvin Harris. 1976. "Population, Warfare, and the Male Supremacist Complex." *American Anthropologist* 78:521–38.

Doolittle, Justus. 1865. *Social Life of the Chinese.* 2 vols. New York: Harper.

Draper, Patricia. 1975. "!Kung Women: Contrasts in Sexual Egalitarianism in Foraging and Sedentary Contexts." In *Toward an Anthropology of Women,* ed. Rayna Reiter. New York: Monthly Review Press.

———. 1976. "Social and Economic Constraints on Child Life among the !Kung." In *Kalahari Hunter-Gatherers,* ed. R. Lee and I. DeVore, pp. 199–217. Cambridge, Mass.: Harvard University Press.

Dunham, Carroll. 1988. "A Marriage in Shambala." 1986 *Geo* (Paris, France), vol. 94: 17–21.

Ember, Carol. 1983. "The Relative Decline in Women's Contribution to Agriculture with Intensification." *American Anthropologist* 85:285–304.

Ember, Carol, Melvin Ember, and Burton Pasternak. 1974. "On the Development of Unilineal Descent." *Journal of Anthropological Research* 30:69–94.

Engels, Friedrich. [1891] 1942. *The Origin of the Family, Private Property, and the State, in the Light of the Researches of Lewis H. Morgan.* New York: International Publishers.

Fenton, William N. 1998. *The Great Law and the Longhouse: A Political History of the Iroquois Confederacy.* Norman: University of Oklahoma Press.

———, ed. 1968. *Parker on the Iroquois.* New York: Syracuse University Press.

Foster, Michael K., Jack Campisi, and Marianne Mithun, eds. 1984. *Extending the Rafters: Interdisciplinary Approaches to Iroquoian Studies.* New York: State University of New York Press.

Freedman, Maurice. 1967. "Ancestor Worship: Two Facets of the Chinese Case." In *Social Organization,* ed. M. Freedman, pp. 85–103. Chicago: University of Chicago Press.

———. 1966. *Chinese Lineage and Society.* London: London School of Economics.

Fried, Morton. 1967. *The Evolution of Political Society.* New York: Random House.

Friedl. Ernestine. 1984. *Women and Men: An Anthropologist's View.* New York: Holt, Rinehart and Winston, 1975. Reprint, Prospect Heights, Ill.: Waveland Press.

Ginsburg, Faye, and Rayna Rapp. 1995. *Conceiving the New World Order: The Global Politics of Reproduction.* Berkeley: University of California Press.

Godelier, Maurice. 1977. *Marxist Perspectives in Anthropology.* Cambridge: Cambridge University Press.

Goldstein, Melvyn. 1976. "Fraternal Polyandry and Fertility in a High Himalayan Valley in Northwest Nepal." *Human Ecology* 4:423–33.

———. 1989. *A History of Modern Tibet, 1913–1951.* Berkeley: University of California Press.

———. 1971. "Stratification, Polyandry, and Family Structure in Central Tibet." *Southwestern Journal of Anthropology* 27:64–74.

———. 1987. "When Brothers Share a Wife." *Natural History,* March, pp. 39–48.

Goode, William J. 1970. *World Revolution and Family Patterns.* New York: Free Press.

Goody, Jack. 1985. *The Oriental, the Ancient, and the Primitive: Systems of Marriage and the Family in the Pre-Industrial Societies of Eurasia.* Cambridge: Cambridge University Press.

Gordon, Robert. 1992. *The Bushman Myth: The Making of a Namibian Underclass.* Boulder, Colo.: Westview.

Harrell, Stevan. 1997. *Human Families.* Boulder, Colo.: Westview.

Harris, Marvin. 1975. *Cows, Pigs, Wars, and Witches: The Riddles of Culture.* New York: Random House.

Herdt, Gilbert. 1992. *Gay Culture in America.* Boston: Beacon Press.

Ho Ping-ti. 1962. *The Ladder of Success in Imperial China: Aspects of Social Mobility, 1368–1911.* New York: Columbia University Press.

Hobsbawm, Eric, and Terrence Ranger, eds. 1983. *The Invention of Tradition.* Cambridge: Cambridge University Press.

Jaschok, Maria. 1988. *Concubines and Bondservants.* Hong Kong: Oxford.

Katz, Richard. 1982. *Boiling Energy: Community Healing among the Kalahari Kung.* Cambridge, Mass.: Harvard University Press.

Klein, Laura F., and Lillian Ackerman, eds. 1995. *Women and Power in Native North America.* Norman: University of Oklahoma Press.

Ko, Dorothy. 1994. *Teachers of the Inner Chambers: Women and Culture in China, 1573–1722.* Stanford, Calif.: Stanford University Press.

Leacock, Eleanor. 1978. "Women's Status in Egalitarian Society: Implications for Social Evolution." *Current Anthropology* 19, no. 2:247–75.

Lee, Richard B. 1993. *The Dobe Ju/'Hoansi,* 2nd ed. New York: Harcourt Brace.

———. 1993. "Eating Christmas in the Kalahari." In *The Dobe Ju/'Hoansi* by R. Lee, 2nd ed., pp. 183–88. New York: Harcourt Brace.

———. 1979. *The !Kung San: Men, Women, and Work in a Foraging Society.* Cambridge: Cambridge University Press.

———. 1981. "Politics, Sexual and Nonsexual, in an Egalitarian Society: The !Kung San." In *Social Inequality,* ed. G. Berreman, pp. 83–101. New York: Academic Press.

Lee, Richard, and Irven DeVore, eds. 1976. *Kalahari Hunter-Gatherers*. Cambridge, Mass.: Harvard University Press.

Lenski, Gerhard. 1966. *Power and Privilege*. New York: McGraw Hill.

Levine, Nancy. 1988. *The Dynamics of Polyandry: Kinship, Domesticity, and Population on the Tibetan Border*. Chicago: University of Chicago Press.

———. 1980. "Nyinba Polyandry and the Allocation of Paternity." *Journal of Comparative Family Studies* 11:283–98.

———. 1980. "Opposition and Interdependence: Demographic and Economic Perspectives on Nyinba Slavery." In *Asian and African Systems of Slavery*, ed. J. L. Watson. Berkeley: University of California Press.

———. 1981. "Perspectives on Love: Morality and Affect in Nyinba Interpersonal Relationships." In *Culture and Morality: Essays in Honor of Christoph von Fürer-Haimendorf*. Delhi: Oxford University Press.

Levine, Nancy, and Joan Silk. 1997. "Why Polyandry Fails: Sources of Instability in Polyandrous Marriages." *Current Anthropology* 38, no. 3:375–88.

Levy, Howard. 1966. *Chinese Footbinding*. Tokyo: Weatherhill.

Lewin, Ellen. 1993. *Lesbian Mothers*. Ithaca: Cornell University Press.

Malinowski, Bronislaw. [1929] 1987. *The Sexual Life of Savages in North-Western Melanesia*. Boston: Beacon Press.

Mann, Susan. 1997. *Precious Records: Women in China's Long Eighteenth Century*. Stanford, Calif.: Stanford University Press.

Marshall, Lorna. 1976. *The !Kung of Nyae Nyae*. Cambridge, Mass.: Harvard University Press.

———. 1976. "Sharing, Talking, and Giving: Relief of Social Tensions among the !Kung." In *Kalahari Hunter-Gatherers*, ed. R. Lee and I. DeVore, pp. 349–72. Cambridge, Mass.: Harvard University Press.

Martinez-Alier, Verena. 1974. *Marriage, Class, and Colour in Nineteenth Century Cuba: A Study of Racial Attitudes and Sexual Values in a Slave Society*. Cambridge: Cambridge University Press.

May, Martha. 1982. "The Historical Problem of the Family Wage." *Feminist Studies* 8, no. 2:399–424.

McC. Netting, Robert, Richard R. Wilk, and Eric J. Arnould, eds. 1984. *Households: Comparative and Historical Studies of the Domestic Group*. Berkeley: University of California Press.

Meillassoux, Claude. 1972. "From Reproduction to Production." *Economy and Society* 1:83–105.

———. 1981. *Maidens, Meal, and Money*. New York: Cambridge University Press.

Moise, Edwin. 1977. "Downward Social Mobility in Pre-Revolutionary China." *Modern China* 3:3–32.

Morgan, Lewis Henry. [1851] 1962. *League of the Ho-de-no-sau-ne, or Iroquois*. New York: Corinth Press.

———. 1877. *Ancient Society*. New York: Henry Holt.

Ortner, Sherry. 1996. "Gender Hegemonies." In *Making Gender: The Politics and Erotics of Culture*, ed. S. Ortner, pp. 139–72. Boston: Beacon Press.

———. 1978. "The Virgin and the State." *Feminist Studies* 4, no. 3:19–35.

Peter, Prince of Greece and Denmark. 1963. *A Study of Polyandry*. The Hague: n.p.

———. 1965. "The Tibetan Family System." In *Comparative Family Systems*, ed. M. F. Nimkoff, pp. 192–208. Boston: Houghton Mifflin.

Potuchek, Jean. 1997. *Who Supports the Family? Gender and Breadwinning in Dual-Earner Marriages.* Stanford, Calif.: Stanford University Press.

Quinn, Naomi. 1977. "Anthropological Studies on Women's Status." *Annual Review of Anthropology* 6:189–90.

Rabinow, Paul. 1977. *Reflections on Fieldwork in Morocco.* Berkeley: University of California Press.

Rapp, Rayna. 1982. "Family and Class in Contemporary America: Notes toward an Understanding of Ideology." In *Rethinking the Family: Some Feminist Questions,* ed. B. Thorne, with M. Yalom, pp. 168–87. New York: Longman.

Richardson, Hugh. 1998. *High Peaks, Pure Earth: Collected Writings on Tibetan History and Culture.* London: Serinda.

Rosaldo, Michelle Z. 1980. "The Use and Abuse of Anthropology: Reflections on Feminism and Cross-Cultural Understanding." *Signs* 5, no. 3:89–417.

———. 1974. "Woman, Culture, and Society: A Theoretical Overview." In *Woman, Culture, and Society,* ed. M. Rosaldo and L. Lamphere. Stanford, Calif.: Stanford University Press.

Rubin, Lillian. 1976. *Worlds of Pain: Life in the Working-Class Family.* New York: Basic Books.

Sahlins, Marshall. 1968. "Culture and Environment: The Study of Cultural Ecology." In *Theory in Anthropology,* ed. R. Manners and D. Kaplan, pp. 367–73. New York: Aldine.

Sanday, Peggy. 1974. "Female Status in the Public Domain." In *Woman, Culture, and Society,* ed. M. Rosaldo and L. Lamphere, pp. 189–206. Stanford, Calif.: Stanford University Press.

Schneider, David. 1980. *American Kinship: A Cultural Account,* 2nd ed. Chicago: University of Chicago Press.

———. 1961. "The Distinctive Features of Matrilineal Descent Groups." In *Matrilineal Kinship,* ed. D. Schneider and K. Gough, pp. 1–29. Berkeley: University of California Press.

Schneider, David, and Kathleen Gough, eds. 1961. *Matrilineal Kinship.* Berkeley: University of California Press.

Service, Elman. 1962. *Primitive Social Organization: An Evolutionary Perspective.* New York: Random House.

Shepherd, John. 1995. *Marriage and Mandatory Abortion among the Seventeenth Century Siraya.* N.p.: American Ethnological Society. Monograph Series, 6.

Shostak, Marjorie. 1981. *Nisa: The Life and Words of a !Kung Woman.* New York: Random House.

Silverblatt, Irene. 1991. "Interpreting Women in States: New Feminist Ethnohistories." In *Gender at the Crossroads,* ed. M. di Leonardo, pp. 140–74. Berkeley: University of California Press.

Skinner, G. William. 1976. "Mobility Strategies in Late Imperial China." In *Regional Analysis,* vol. 1, ed. C. Smith, pp. 327–64. New York: Academic Press.

Spindler, George, ed. 1997. *Education and Cultural Process: Anthropological Approaches.* 3rd ed. Prospect Heights, Ill.: Waveland Press.

Spittal, W. G. 1990. *Iroquois Women: An Anthology.* Ontario: Iroqrafts.

Stacey, Judith. 1990. Brave New Families: Stories of Domestic Upheaval in Late Twentieth Century America. New York: Basic Books.

Stack, Carol. 1974. All Our Kin: Strategies for Survival in a Black Community. New York: Harper Row.

Stein, R. A. 1972. *Tibetan Civilization*. Stanford, Calif.: Stanford University Press.
Stockard, Janice E. 1989. *Daughters of the Canton Delta: Marriage Patterns and Economic Strategies in South China, 1860–1930*. Stanford, Calif.: Stanford University Press.
———. 2000. "Reeling Silk and Identity in Natal Homes: Residence, Labor, and the Production of Daughters in South China." Paper presented at the 99th Annual Meeting of the American Anthropological Association, November.
Stocking, George. 1982. "Franz Boas and the Culture Concept in Historical Perspective." In *Race, Culture, and Evolution: Essays in the History of Anthropology*, ed. G. Stocking, pp. 195–233. Chicago: University of Chicago Press.
Thomas, Elizabeth Marshall. 1989. *The Harmless People*. 2nd ed. New York: Random House.
———. 1987. *Reindeer Moon*. Boston: Houghton Mifflin.
Tooker, Elizabeth. 1978. "The League of the Iroquois: Its History, Politics, and Ritual." In *Handbook of North American Indians*. Vol. 15, *Northeast*, ed. B. Trigger, pp. 418–41. Washington D.C.: Smithsonian Institution.
———. 1984. "Women in Iroquois Society." In *Extending the Rafters: Interdisciplinary Approaches to Iroquoian Studies*, ed. M. Foster, J. Campisi, and M. Mithun, pp. 109–23. Albany: State University of New York.
Topley, Marjorie. 1975. "Marriage Resistance in Rural Kwangtung." In *Women in Chinese Society*, ed. M. Wolf and R. Witke, pp. 67–88. Stanford, Calif.: Stanford University Press.
Trautman, Thomas. 1987. *Lewis Henry Morgan and the Invention of Kinship*. Berkeley: University of California Press.
Turner, Christine. 1997. "Locating Footbinding: Variations across Class and Space in Nineteenth and Early Twentieth Century China. *Journal of Historical Sociology* 10, no. 4:444–79.
Underhill, Ruth. 1956. *The Navajos*. Norman: University of Oklahoma Press.
Verdon, Michel. 1998. *Rethinking Households: An Atomistic Perspective on European Living Arrangements*. London: Routledge.
Wallace, Anthony. 1970. *The Death and Rebirth of the Seneca*. New York: Knopf.
Watson, James L. 1975. *Emigration and the Chinese Lineage: The Mans in Hong Kong and London*. Berkeley: University of California Press.
———. 1980. "Transactions in People: The Chinese Market in Slaves, Servants, and Heirs." In *Asian and African Systems of Slavery*, ed. J.L. Watson. Oxford: Basil Blackwell.
Watson, Rubie. 1985. *Inequality among Brothers: Class and Kinship in South China*. Cambridge: Cambridge University Press.
———. 1991. "Wives, Concubines, and Maids: Servitude and Kinship in the Hong Kong Region, 1900–1940." In *Marriage and Inequality in Chinese Society*, ed. R. Watson and P. Ebrey, pp. 231–55. Berkeley: University of California Press.
Watson, Rubie, and Patricia Ebrey, eds. 1991. *Marriage and Inequality in Chinese Society*. Berkeley: University of California Press.
Weiner, Annette. 1978. "Trobriand Kinship from Another View: The Reproductive Power of Women and Men." *Man* 14:328–48.
———. 1988. *The Trobrianders of Papua New Guinea*. New York: Holt, Rinehart and Winston.
———. 1976. *Women of Value, Men of Renown*. Austin: University of Texas.
Weston, Kath. 1991. *Families We Choose: Lesbians, Gays, Kinship*. New York: Columbia University Press.

Wolf, Arthur. 1974. "Gods, Ghosts, and Ancestors." In *Religion and Ritual in Chinese Society*, ed. A. Wolf, pp. 131–82. Stanford, Calif.: Stanford University Press.

———. 1981. *Marriage and Adoption in China, 1845–1945*. Stanford, Calif.: Stanford University Press.

Wolf, Margery. 1972. *Women and the Family in Rural Taiwan*. Stanford, Calif.: Stanford University Press.

Yanagisako, Sylvia, and Jane Collier. 1987. "Toward a Unified Analysis of Gender and Kinship." In *Gender and Kinship: Essays toward a Unified Analysis*, ed. J. Collier and S. Yanagisako, pp. 1–50. Stanford, Calif.: Stanford University Press.

Yang, Martin C. 1945. *A Chinese Village*. New York: Columbia University Press.

Yellen, John. 1990. "The Transformation of the Kalahari !Kung." *Scientific American* 262, no. 4:96–105.

Index

References to figures are printed in italics.

Brideservice
  defined, 15
  among !Kung San, 15, 20, 28–33,
    110 n6
Bridewealth and dowry
  in China, 38–39, 47, *56*
  defined, 47
  among Nyinba, 88–89, 93, 96

China
  class stratification, 8–9, 38–40
  kinship and family
    male ancestor worship, 43–44,
      47–50, 113 n13
    male descent line, 9, 43, 46, 113
      n13, 113 n15
    and place of females in, 48–50
    lineages, 46, 113 n14
    patrilineal kinship, 43–46, 48–50
  marriage
    major marriage
      defined, 44–45, 47
      arrangement, 44, 46–47

  bridewealth and dowry, 38–39,
    47, 56
  polygyny, 10, 53–56, 113 n21
  residence practice, 37, 48, 51–53,
    60
  spirit marriage, 49–50, 113 n17
  See also Delayed transfer marriage
  plow agriculture, 40–43
Class stratification
  in China, 36, 38–40, 53
  and classless societies, 36
  among Nyinba, 88, 89
Collier, Jane 9, 108 n12, 109 n20, 110 n6
Culture, concept of, 2, 4

Delayed transfer marriage
  description, 3–5
  residence practice, 7, 48
  and silk industry, 4
  spatial distribution, 3–5, 113 n16
Doolittle, Reverend Justice
  on Chinese marriage, 38–39, 44
Dowry. *See* Bridewealth and dowry

Egalitarian, 10, 15
  defined, 15–16
  among !Kung San, 15–16, 36, 102
  Iroquois, 60
Engels, Friedrich, 61, 114 n5

Family wage ideology, 68, 105, 117 n1
Fenton, William, viii, 67, 68, 72, 75, 76,
    77, 78
Fieldwork. See Methods
Footbinding, 43, 113 n12
Foraging. See Hunting and gathering

Generalized reciprocity
  defined, 23
  and !Kung San, 23–25, 28, 108 n11

Horticulture, 41–42, 60
  and Iroquois, 65
Hunting and gathering and !Kung San,
    13, 16–18, 25, 28, 40–41

Interviewing. See Methods
Iroquois
  horticulture, 65
  kinship and family, 65, 69
    female descent line, 65–66
    lineage and clan, 65–66, 69–70
    matrilineal kinship, 60, 65–66,
      69–70, 79–80, 115 n11
  marriage
    arrangement of, 58
    residence practice, 59; 65–66, 69,
      72–74, 80
  rank stratification, 60, 70
  spatial distribution, 59–61

Kelly, Thomas, viii, 84, 85, 89, 91, 92,
    94, 95, 96, 97
!Kung San
  bands, 8, 18–22
  brideservice, 20, 28–33, 110 n5 and n6
  divorce, 34–36
  egalitarian relations, 15–16, 30
  generalized reciprocity, 23–25, 28
  hunting and gathering, 13, 16–18, 25,
    28, 40–41
  kinship and family, 11, 18–22

marriage
  arrangement of, 13–14, 28–30
  and hunting, 20, 28–33
  residence practice, 29, 33–34
  spatial distribution, 13–14

Levine, Nancy
  on the Nyinba, 81, 115 n1, 116 n2
Lee, Richard
  on the !Kung San, 24

Marriage
  Gendered analyses of, 5, 108 n11
  See also China; Iroquois; !Kung San;
    Nyinba
Marshall, John, viii
Marshall, Laurence, viii
Marshall family collection, viii, 18, 19,
    20, 21, 31, 35, 36
Marx, Karl, 61
Matrilocal residence
  defined, 69
  effects on marriage and gender, 10,
    59–60, 69, 74, 79
  Iroquois, 60, 69, 74, 79, 80
Methods, ethnographic
  described, 2–4, 107 n3
  fieldwork, 2–3
  interviewing, 3–4, 108 n6
  life history, 2–3
  participant observation, 2
Monogamy
  and !Kung San, 10
  and polyandry among Nyinba, 10, 93,
    96–97
  and polygyny among Chinese, 10
Morgan, Lewis Henry
  on Iroquois, 61, 114 n4
  and kinship, 70

Neolocal residence
  effects on marriage and gender, 106
  in U.S.A., 7–8, 106
Nyinba
  bridewealth and dowry, 88–89, 93, 96
  class stratification, 88, 98
  divorce, 96–97
  kinship and family, 84, 86–87, 89–92, 95

marriage
  arrangement of, 88
  monogamy, 93; 96–97
  polyandry, 10, 80, 81–83, 88, 90,
    93, 97
  polygyny, 95–96
  residence practice, 83–84, 87, 104
  plow agriculture, 83–84, 87

Parker, Ely S., 61
Participant observation. *See* Methods
Patrilocal residence
  in China, 37, 48, 51–53, 60
  defined, 85
  effects on marriage and gender, 51–53,
    84, 86, 103
  among Nyinba, 80, 84
Plow agriculture, 40, 41–43, 83–84, 87
Polyandry (fraternal)
  defined, 10
  and Nyinba, 10, 80, 82, 88, 90, 93, 97
Polygyny
  in China, 53–56
  defined, 10
  among !Kung San, 33
  among Nyinba, 95–96

Rank stratification. *See* Iroquois
Residence practice (postmarital), 7–8, 10,
    109 n21
  Matrilocal, effects on marriage and
    gender, 10, 59–60, 69
  neolocal 7–8, effects on marriage and
    gender, 10, 106
  patrilocal, effects on marriage and gen-
    der, 51–53, 84–86, 103
  uxorilocal 29, effects on marriage and
    gender, 33–35, 102
  virilocal, 34
  See also China; Iroquois; !Kung San;
    Nyinba; U.S.A.

Sedan chairs
  in Chinese marriage, 47, 51
Sericulture. *See* silk industry
Silk industry
  China, 3–5
  and delayed transfer marriage,
    3–5, 49–50, 107 n5,
    108 n9
Slaves
  and marriage among Nyinba, 88,
    97–99, 116 n9
Speck, Frank, viii, *71*

Thomas, Elizabeth Marshall
  on !Kung San, 12–13, 109 n1,
    110 n5
Thomson, John Stuart, vii, *48, 49*
Tibet. *See* Nyinba

United States of America
  family wage ideology, 68, 105–106,
    117 n1
  kinship, 106
  marriage practice, 106
  residence practice, 7–8, 106
Uxorilocal residence
  defined, 29
  effects on marriage and gender, 33–35,
    102
  !Kung San, 29
  See also Matrilocal residence

Virilocal residence, 34

Warfield, James, vii, *53, 54, 55*
Wolf, Margery
  on uterine family (China), 52–53, 113
    n20

Yanagisako, Sylvia, 9, 108 n12, 109
    n20